The Adventure of Sobriety

THE
ADVENTURE
OF
SOBRIETY

DAVID A. STEWART

MICHIGAN STATE UNIVERSITY PRESS

1976

Copyright © *1976*
MICHIGAN STATE UNIVERSITY PRESS
Library of Congress Card Catalog Number: 76–8601
ISBN: 0–87013–199–0
Manufactured in the United States of America

Contents

Acknowledgements

The fellowship of A.A. has had more influence on this study than I can well express.

Lyle Blair and Jean Busfield encouraged me to put a series of lectures into book form. Aileen Brothers ably guided me through the preparation of the manuscript for the press.

D.A.S.

Introduction

Addiction used to mean "devotion." In recent use it is blind devotion in the form of disorder. The addict comes in several forms—the leaner, the schemer, the loner, the drug abuser, as well as the alcoholic. I have singled out the alcoholic for special attention because of my familiarity with the problem, both as an alcoholic and a therapist, and also because the alcoholic demonstrates most of the trouble that can be detected in all other types of addictions.

If you are an alcoholic, you began drinking with a good reason. You wanted to feel free and easy, adventurous and amiable. Not until you move into the problem stage are you bent on the competing urges to feeling good—comfort, satisfaction, and safety—the pleasurable feelings pursued by the leaner, schemer, loner, and drug abuser. Tragically, the pursuit of comfort, satisfaction, and safety ends in anxiety, depression, and loneliness.

Drinking falls into an addictive pattern when it first loses its creative spark and then its power to give comfort, satisfaction, and safety. The habit continues senselessly to dominate your life as an alcoholic from a source deeper and stronger than will power or any other form of control. You depend more desperately than ever on the substance that first gave you meaning but now, at best, gives only sodden unity. The closest you can come to the at-oneness of your early drinking days is deep intoxication, followed by harrowing conflicts, pain, and fearful isolation.

The core of all distress in the drinking habit is that you operate alone. Trying to break, modify, or control the habit only intensifies the problem. In the long run, such behaviors do nothing to bring release or joy.

Temporary abstinence or controlled drinking gives a deceptive appearance of "recovery." After several weeks or months of "white knuckle" sobriety, slips occur, relapses flourish. The number of alcoholics dry by will power, by behavior modification techniques, and other controls is low, if indeed the abstinence or control lasts more than two years. Eventually all methods that isolate the habit and prepare it for attack, confrontation, or control usually fail.

If you could move from one habit to another as easily as you can move from one thought to another, there would be no problem of addiction. The truth is that once an alcoholic always an alcoholic. You cannot think your way out of addiction by a moral rule, by fear of death, or by a set of controls. At best, you can find a creative way to express your addiction.

Your addiction is not something you have, something that by implication you can "dis-have," disown, get rid of, control, or modify. Your being addicted is something you *are*. Drunk or sober, you are an alcoholic. The one feature of your addiction you can do nothing about is this: you cannot drink. You simply have to accept that truth.

However, you can do something about the really meaningful feature of your alcoholism—the longing to feel good. The desire to drink, even in fear, means the desire to feel good. Purged of fear, the desire to feel good will mean the desire to feel good without drinking. Thus, the desire to feel good will at last mean the desire to stop drinking.

If you stop drinking, you do it *best* and *easiest* for the same good reason you first drank. What is the secret of the creative way to discipline alcoholism? It is to accept the habit and join with others where the original design of the habit is fulfilled in fellowship.

By not drinking and by practicing the principles of Alcoholics Anonymous, you can become a *better* alcoholic. In so doing you embark on an adventure in sobriety, freedom, and a more creative way of living.

Allen, now sober for twenty-seven years, is a good example of an alcoholic who found a personal design for living in the A.A. program. Here is his story:

> I used to drink to feel good. In fact, feeling good was my dream, my goal. My original intention was great. It still is. I wanted to be free and easy, adventurous and romantic. And alcohol did that for me—at the start.

> When I was well into the drinking routine, I began to feel a conflict between my dream and the problems of everyday life. The real addiction was my dream, not the alcohol. Of course, I had grown dependent on alcohol, and I prized my drinking as a means to my goal. But, in the conflict stage, a struggle arose between my urge to feel good and the fear that drinking would make me sick. Drink made me feel good. Drink made me feel bad.

> In the control, or alcohol-fighting, stage of my disorder I became anxious, depressed, withdrawn—the opposite of what I really wanted to be. Still I went right on drinking, overcome by the addictive power of alcohol. The positive lesson of addiction I had yet to learn: that the only way to be relieved of the misery of addiction is to become absti-

nent. Simply stop drinking. Addiction never gives a person a parole in terms of control.

Alcohol became the be-all and end-all of my life, even though I knew full well how miserable it could make me most of the time. Any control I exercised was at best only a weak expression of my desire to drink.

After a few years of drinking I knew that I had a real problem. Yet I went on drinking more than ever. I knew better but I did the opposite. Why? I don't have the whole answer. But now I do know this: operating by yourself, making decisions by yourself, is a chronically fearful enterprise. It leads to the rise of self-control and self-sufficiency. Worst of all, to live alone by one's *self-design* is a deeply deceptive way of life. An ego-oriented life style puts control in first place. So I went on for years guided by the control method. I persisted in it long after it failed to bring me release because I knew no other way.

Finally, I found the right key when I picked up the *personal design* for living in discipline among others like myself. A.A. taught me to accept my disorder, not fight it. A.A. members put themselves in each other's place and break the circle that imprisons each in his separate ego, struggling for control. In place of control, A.A. members exercise discipline, a loving regard for one another. A.A.'s *personal design* for living gives me everything, and even more, than I wanted when I drank in the good old days.

Like a million alcoholics all over the world, Allen has drawn from the wisdom and insight of Alcoholics Anonymous in making a creative way of life for himself. What is Alcoholics Anonymous, familiarly known as A.A., and what wisdom does it share that is not found in any current system of science, religion, or art?

Alcoholics Anonymous

Alcoholics Anonymous is a fellowship of alcoholics— men and women who, powerless over alcohol, find their lives to be unmanageable by themselves. Members are anonymous in that each is known by his identity as an alcoholic, not by his reputation, prestige, financial standing, or place in society. In meetings where first names suffice, anonymous comes to mean informal, free, simply structured.

Here is how Alcoholics Anonymous explains itself and its purposes:

> Alcoholics Anonymous is a fellowship of men and women who share their experience, strength and hope with each other that they may solve their common problem and help others to recover from alcoholism.
>
> The only requirement for membership is a desire to stop drinking. There are no dues or fees for A.A. membership; we are self-supporting through our own contributions.
>
> A.A. is not allied with any sect, denomination, politics, organization or institution; does not wish to engage in any controversy, neither endorses nor opposes any causes.
>
> Our primary purpose is to stay sober and help other alcoholics to achieve sobriety.

The newcomer to A.A. is invited to declare that he is powerless over alcohol and that his life is unmanageable, if he can. In the typical A.A. story the new member may well infer that the way he used to be is a portion of his story that is as acceptable as the finish, his freedom in fellowship. Fellow A.A. members accept the newcomer just as he is, was, or will be.

Since problem drinking is self-oriented, it cannot exist in true fellowship. However, the unmanageable life can belong in fellowship, which does not operate on any kind of controls. Fellowship flourishes in personal discipline, the need for one another in love and shared experience.

Basic to the A.A. program are the personal story and group discussion, guided by a set of steps, traditions, slogans, and several prayers. A.A. has also published several books, including *Alcoholics Anonymous, The Twelve Steps and Twelve Traditions, A.A. Comes of Age,* and *As Bill Sees It.* It also publishes the monthly *Grapevine* and many pamphlets on a wide variety of problems related to drinking and alcoholism. A recent biography of Bill W., a cofounder, is also available.*

This study is an effort to support the A.A. way of life in all branches of its philosophy—in Alanon, in Alateen, as well as in A.A. itself. The study uses a three-phase approach, the time-tested technique of A.A. speakers: what it used to be like, what happened, and what it is like now.

The opinions expressed are not to be attributed either to any A.A. group or to A.A. as a whole. They are, in sum, my views as a student. I believe that what I say is in harmony with the principles and practices of A.A.

The fact that I have applied much of the content profes-

*All publications are available by writing to A.A. World Services Inc., P.O. Box 459, Grand Central Station, New York, N.Y. 10017.

sionally makes it essential to distinguish it from A.A. as practiced in A.A. groups throughout the world. However, it is my fervent hope that some A.A. members and some professionals might find it useful in their twelfth step efforts. This study is certainly not intended as a replacement of A.A. At best, it may be regarded as a bridge into A.A. if other efforts have failed.

The A.A. philosophy has reached at least five million people in their various problems with the challenges of living. If this study helps make A.A. more attractive to some of the millions who still suffer, I will feel deeply grateful that the effort was worthwhile.

Chapter 1

The Unanonymous World

The Having Life Style

The unanonymous world is bent merely on having, on satisfying human desires. It is the competitive, aggressive struggle of the workaday world, where we are overdriven by urges of success, convinced that personal meaning is based on occupation or profession. It is a commitment to success as known in wealth and prestige.

Our human desires are chiefly concerned with the pursuit of money, power, sex, and all associated activities. These desires are essential but should never be goals by themselves. They are instrumental to the experiences of personal life. They serve the need *to be*—to be free, to be creative, to be loving.

However, when we seek to satisfy our human desires for their own sake, we become enslaved by those desires. We limit our life style to self-concern, losing sight of our personal longing for the great adventure, the secret of life not found in the workaday world. Money, power, and sex by themselves, at best, breed half-persons, human beings who fail to realize their personal nature in the experience of love. Human desires become love disorders when they fail to complete their course in contact with other individuals in pursuit of personal meaning.

People easily fall into patterns of fear formed around problems posed by money, power, and sex and the urges of ownership, control, and conquest that symbolize them. When the general philosophy of *having,* instead of *being,* predominates, the fearful self, lacking personal discipline, turns to techniques of control to secure a variety of havings in search of some meaning. These control techniques include blame placing, manipulation, and withdrawal, all of which may be termed *dry addictions.* Quite a number of dry addicts easily fall into problem drinking and drug abuse.

Many of us are still caught up in the delusion that the only meaningful experiences are power plays, or control techniques, which, of course, must always be accurate. "Accurate" presumably means measurable in quantitative terms. This is what I call the *quantity dogma.* It flourishes not only among experts but also among active alcoholics and other addicts. On the other hand, creative people who know how to love may not always be accurate but they are always authentic.

In the unanonymous world we tend to judge the worth of life in terms of pleasure, of how much we satisfy our desires. In so doing, we seek to avoid pain. For example, the drinking routine is marked early by the pursuit of comfortable feelings and the avoidance of pain.

The Possession Principle

Those of us who pursue pleasure, avoid pain, and seek power are governed by the *possession principle,* and we suffer from a love disorder. We possess or have and at the some time are possessed or "had."

By themselves, pleasure, pain, and power are inadequate measures of healthy living. To restrict ourselves to
the pursuit of pleasure or power and avoidance of pain is
to cultivate only our self-feelings, and to neglect our personal meaning. To concentrate only on our self-feelings is
to breed anxiety and self-pity, resentment and depression, elation and aloneness. To think only of ourselves is
to destroy ourselves.

Measured by the possession principle and quantity
dogma, we may expect to find people disillusioned and
cynical about life. And we do. Among us are those who are
bored, weary, and disdainful of life in most of its forms.
More concerned with what they possess or control than
with what they are, they can find nothing meaningful,
nothing new. They see nothing wonderful in their daily
rounds. They become anxious. They grow disturbed.
They cease to be interested in living but feel threatened
by death.

Yet the all-pervasive urge to live is so strong that a
distaste for life, no matter how deep, cannot overcome it.
For any meaning that the desire to die can have is itself
derived from life! If the suicidal person were consistent in
his dislike of life, he would try to learn how to die effectively. But to do this is precisely what it means to live
abundantly!

Our involvement in life is so complete that the question
of its worth, itself a living act, can end in only one way:
"That life is worth living is the most necessary of assump-
tions, and were it not assumed the most impossible of
conclusions," as George Santayana has expressed it so
well.

The worth of life cannot be justified if we depend sim-

ply on a calculus of pleasure against pain. Such a calcula-
tion is actually false to the facts of human experience.
Every experience of value is a complex mixture of danger,
mystery, pain, pleasure, and knowledge. When this is well
understood, we learn that the worth of life is judged not
by a rational analysis of pleasure against pain but by a
relishing of experience for its adventure value, come what
may.

In place of pleasure, pain, and power as the standards,
we choose to take up the standards of freedom and sense
of limits. *To be free, and to know where our freedom stops,
will be to experience what it is to be personal.*

The force that makes us most skeptical of living, most
likely to doubt its worth, is fear. Now fear has its limited
value; in normal concern, it is healthy evidence of self-
preservation. However, when self-concern grows excessive, fear becomes unhealthy, and it is in this sense I use
the word here. Fear enslaves us when we fail to understand it and fail to reduce it. We question the worth of life
in the degree to which we fear, and depending on how
long we remain in the fear situation.

Fear is a desire in reverse. We want what we are afraid
of. A desire is a form of fear if the desire is for something
we cannot be or have, like wanting a drink if we are
alcoholics. We can only desire, freely and productively,
what we are capable of being or having.

Desires and Problems They Create

As indicated, our human desires are chiefly concerned
with the pursuit of money, power, sex. They are, in general, the expression of the human will. When the human
will does not serve what we may call the personal will—

the urge to be a free, creative, loving human being—and when the human will is considered as an end in itself, we can get into all sorts of trouble.

Human desires create problems for three main reasons: (1) even the fullest satisfaction of them always leaves still more to be desired; (2) the frustration of them leaves a depressing sense of incompleteness; and (3) they point to conquest and sufficiency, which isolate an individual, making him fearful and lonely. It is on the basis of these three problems that we are constantly exploited in countless ways by other people and by ourselves.

The person caught in the pattern of human desires sees people and things only in relation to his own deep, fearful needs. Pining for this ideal conformity of everything to the pattern of his desires, he keeps expecting wonderful events to befall him. But the sating of human desires for their own sake brings only a boring experience of imitation.

All of us at some time in our lives have been caught up in the problems of human desires, which may be roughly classified into three types of disordered self-feeling: anxiety, depression, and loneliness or self-sufficiency. The drinker experiences these self-feelings long before he becomes a full-fledged alcoholic. I will briefly describe how you behave when you are afflicted by them.

Anxiety. You are restless. A glance in the mirror reflects a lined, worried face. In the course of a challenging task the palms of your hands perspire, though the room is cool. Perhaps you may catch yourself biting off ragged nails. Your pulse may trip along merrily as if it were stumbling. The pupils of your eyes may take on a mild staring aspect. As you worry about trivial problems, you find it hard to relax, and sleep does not come easily. Too concerned about yourself, you find it hard to get any fun out of life or any satisfaction from what you do. This excessive self-concern interferes with your work. A vague need to be protected may dimly call to mind that your mother, or someone else, always made the comforting final decisions about what you should do, as you moved from one crisis to the next in the long overextended period of your adolescence.

This experience may be disturbing to look at when you see it for the first time. But when you look at it again, you notice something wonderfully relieving. It begins to be detached from you. You can take another look at it, and that examination gives you some clues about yourself that you had never known before. When you give the self-feeling a name, anxiety, you begin to discipline it. And the first best technique you can use is to have a good laugh at this worried character—you. When you do that, you take most of the load off a fellow trying to support the whole world on his slumping shoulders—a world of your own. You discover that self-pity is the forerunner of anxiety, and anxiety is not far from feelings of guilt. You have become a leaner and have developed a habit of blame placing.

Depression. You feel sad and low. It is difficult to get through the day's work, not because you are lazy but because you do not seem to have the energy. As you walk, your shoulders droop. You glance downward, watching your feet, and your strides are short and languid. You may notice that your arms are not swinging. When you turn your head, your whole body turns as though you were one rigid piece. If your depressed state lasts more than a day, you awaken early in the morning before the end of a normal night's sleep. At meals you eat mechanically, with poor appetite. A sense of guilt may haunt you, and you tend to want to cry. You are disturbed from time to time by sexual fantasies and seem to regress to childish or youthful needs.

Periodically you experience a strong sense of elation, an overcompensation for the feeling of depression. The habit of overexpectancy that you cultivate during elation leads you into patterns of manipulation. If you become a schemer as a result of your control urges, you will, of course, suffer from eventual depression. Resentment is a common forerunner to depression, and from depression it is not too far to despair.

Within such a fog, you may pause and ask, "Is life worth living?" If you are aware you are depressed, you will be in a position to do something about it. So you will avoid making judgments of others or important decisions until you are out of your depression.

The most certain fact you can be sure of is that a depressed state will not last. Everyone from time to time goes through disappointments and therefore is likely to feel depressed. The whole problem is to do something about it. The easiest, quickest way out of a depression is to talk with someone whose problems are like yours. When you show another troubled person that you understand him, your guilt will disappear and you will rediscover that life is worth living.

Self-Sufficiency. When you are elated, you are overactive, feeling so good you cannot stand it. Your mind trickles over with one idea after another, and no task seems too great for your capacities. You begin many things and finish few. Still you greet serious tasks with a patronizing laugh and regard a big job as a mere detail. The actual doing of the job awaits you around a corner you never turn.

During an elated period your overconfidence is not deflated by any prospect of the inability to measure up to your pretensions. You are so insecure in your happiness that you feel compelled to bring others to your aid in celebrating a pleasant event, on your terms, in a possessive, controlling way. Expansive and grandiose, you seek to impress others with your good fortune and boundless happiness. The drinks are on you, but you call the tune and put others in your debt.

Elation is not as pleasurable as it looks. It has an inner core of deep uneasiness and growing fear. The happy manic state eventually dips into a depression, and then into a desperate urge to be self-sufficient, since you suspect that this insecure pleasure is neither authentic nor enduring.

The forerunner of elation is a sense of inadequacy, closely related to subsequent feelings of depression. Then you are not far from the isolation of self-sufficiency, which is fearful and uneasy. Self-sufficiency is a temporary delusion in which, letting your fancy roam, you imagine yourself to be supremely right, powerful, and self-contained. Disaster is just around the corner.

Whenever anything goes wrong, you seek recovery in authority you can respect or in will power you believe you ought to exercise. Tragically, both recovery and will power are the same form as your old isolated misery.

Your great need is to rise above mere recovery and grim will power to creative living and relaxing joy. Till then you suffer from a chronic sense of inadequacy. You can never be self-sufficient enough to be confident, care-free, and happy. Though occasionally manic, appearing to be happy, your collapse in regression to a depressed state is soon to take place.

This collapse is due to your disillusionment with the first two defenses. You discover that neither leaning on others nor trying to impress them is of any use at all. You live unto yourself, fearful of anything foreign to your familiar ways. The result of the self-sufficiency habit is to become chronically lonely, desperately in need of love. You become a loner.

The remedy for self-sufficiency is the same as that for anxiety and depression. You note the signs, become aware of the disordered self-feeling, and understand it to be a disturbed state in need of discipline. Then you need to find someone as disturbed as yourself and try to understand that person in terms of his feelings. It is important to put yourself in the place of another in order to understand your own feelings.

Leaner, Schemer, and Loner

Anxiety, depression, and self-sufficiency—the disordered self-feelings of the leaner, schemer, and loner—are forms of self-intoxication. The intoxication deepens if we do not take steps to undergo personal sobering up.

The leaner suffers from "people" addiction, and the loner is afflicted with the "tenderness taboo." The conflict between people addiction and the tenderness taboo is the conflict between the symbol Money and the symbol Sex.

Money symbolizes dependence (debt), anxiety, guilt. "Debt" is illustrated in the traits of the leaner. He tends to fasten on to people in his deep need to find his identity in them. His separation fear, dependence, and anxiety eventually lead to guilt. The entire pattern is marked by the habit of blame placing.

Sex symbolizes the opposite tendency to that of Money. The same person, the leaner, in his fear of commitment pulls away from people in a reactive urge to be self-sufficient. Sex problems flourish in this loner, due to his fear of commitment, the fear of intimacy imposed by the tenderness taboo. Self-importance comes to be based on self-sufficiency, with eventual fearful loneliness.

Power is shown in the tension between Money and Sex. Here we find the schemer—he who is urged to compromise between money problems and sex drives. What satisfaction he fails to secure from money and sex he seeks in power or prestige. The schemer, worn by the struggle, grows depressed, tense. His depression results from the habit of manipulating or controlling either himself or others, and it eventuates in despair.

Blame placing is debit placing; it draws attention to oneself in self-pity. Controlling or being controlled is a power game; it singles the individual out in his resentments. Withdrawal may involve stress on sex without commitment; it marks the person in his desperate self-sufficiency and loneliness. All three patterns are expressions of "having" and "being had."

Despair is likely to be the lot of anyone suffering from an overpowering defect. But such a person can take heart in the time-tested truth that no courage is so great as that born in complete desperation. It is desperate people who qualify well for adventure. The tragedy of life is not found in despair but in indifference and complacency.

Self-feeling disorders are love disorders because they illustrate alienation from others, the absence of love. Freedom from such a disorder is always found in a source other than the actual location of the disorder. The source of freedom has to be higher and more complex than the trouble itself. For example, if you chew your nails or your hands perspire—signs of anxiety—you do not remove the discomfort by bandaging your fingers or by using skin lotion. Such aids may alleviate the trouble briefly, but are inadequate treatments because they do not go to the proper source of the trouble. They are only physical means of dealing with a psychological problem. You cannot cure the higher by treating the lower. You cannot overcome a complex problem by a simple solution.

A physical disorder calls merely for the control of pain and the restoration of the healthy working of the impaired area. But personal disorders represent an enslavement to human desires, a seeking of pleasure and avoidance of pain. Freedom from such disorders therefore requires the discipline of both pain and pleasure. Pleasure needs to be disciplined if it is not to become pain in the form of boredom, anxiety, depression, or elation.

The discipline of pain and pleasure does not take its source in either pain or pleasure. It originates elsewhere —in the form and balance created in the interplay of you with others, an interpersonal art.

The Being Life Style

Ironically, all three areas symbolized by money, power, and sex are cultivated in response to three perfectly sound thirsts: "I need you," "I anticipate good things," and "I want to be meaningful (I am important)." Thus, it is as leaners, schemers, and loners that we are qualified to become agents, artists, and friends, which represent the *being* life style. There is no real opposition between the personal disturbance and the ideal outcome. They are correlative, not opposed.

The real adventurer, the person who rises above love disorders, is he who knows that new and strange experiences do not just happen in accordance with human desires alone. Those experiences come about through his own energy in concert with others in pursuit of personal ideals. Others are needed as partners in this adventure.

A desire in full flower becomes a personal feeling involving others. It is always disciplined by a purpose, to be expressed creatively. It always has due regard for anyone or anything else it is likely to involve.

The leaner, schemer, and loner, as well as the alcoholic, move from their trouble into their destiny as persons by giving themselves over to good will in the activities of fellowship. This is what it means *to be* rather than to be "had."

Chapter 2

The Meaning of Our Drinking

Intention, Technique, and Outcome

Every action consists of an intention, a technique, and an outcome or practice. Every intention consists of a purpose and a desire. The desire is directed by the purpose to a creative practice or to a distressing one. The practice will be creative if the purpose is "to be." It will be distressing if the purpose is lost to the desire "to have."

Together, intention, technique, and practice make up a guiding principle. For example, dependence, control, ego, alcoholism, prestige are guiding principles of the having life style. (See page 85 for principles of the being life style.)

If your guiding principle is dependence, you are a leaner. Your intention is to depend on other people, to avoid responsibility. Thereby you develop the technique of blame placing. The outcome is self-pity, anxiety, and guilt feelings. (The outline of other guiding principles is shown in Table 1.)

Dependence, control, and ego are often observed in those whose guiding principle is either alcoholism or prestige. The outcomes of all five principles are familiar and

Table 1

GUIDING PRINCIPLES OF HAVING LIFE STYLES

Principle	Intention	Technique	Outcome
Dependence (Leaner)	to have people to depend on, to avoid responsibility	blame placing	self-pity, anxiety, guilt
Control (Schemer)	to manipulate other people or oneself	overexpectant control, various "cons"	resentment, depression, despair
Ego (Loner)	to have an "image," to have people for use at a distance	withdrawal	isolation, loneliness, fear of the foreign, authoritative outlook
Alcoholism	to feel good	drinking and the use of dependence, control, and self-sufficiency	miserable, ugly, afraid, sick
Prestige	to gain credit and recognition, to be well regarded	role playing, politics	chronic fear of disfavor and loss of status

do not match the original intentions. To discipline these principles is to become aware that their intentions are those of having.

The word "thirst" (longing) well expresses the urgency of a desire as well as the continuity between the desire and its object. If we thirst for something, we do well to accept the longing and try to fulfill it. It is ruinous to deny it by cure or suppression.

The principle of acceptance is important. If the thirst leads to alcohol, we should accept and respect what we want. What we want can be creatively integrated into a sobriety program. The best feature of drinking is syner-

gized with the sobriety purpose. Love, as known in fellowship, will be the technique that replaces the bottle. But
the purpose, or reason, for drinking is retained and
blended into the sober way of life. That reason, of course,
is to feel good.

Before we examine the meaning of our drinking, let us
look at the stages of the drinking pattern.

The Drinking Pattern

If an outcome matches our intention, we have a sound
meaning, a sound action. Otherwise, of course, the meaning is unsound; the action means frustration, a denial of
self, a working against self.

Problem drinking begins with good intentions that become defective. The original intentions are to feel good,
to be free, to be companionable.

Alcoholism is an addiction, a process of slavery, first
conceived in the interest of pleasure. We can think of
addiction in terms of inhibition. The three forms of inhibition are support, control, and surrender—traits of the
leaner, schemer, and loner.

In the five stages of the drinking pattern the alcoholic
experiences the need for all three forms of inhibition.
(This drinking pattern can be extended five more stages
into sobriety, as I shall explain in Chapter 4.)

1. *Dream Drinking.* In this stage the desire to drink is
really a desire for love. As dream drinkers we long to be
free, easy, adventurous, and friendly. In time, drinking
becomes a design for living, a way to cope with every joy,
every sadness, every frustration. It becomes a technique
that applies to everything in our lives.

In order to develop this technique, this art, we have to
develop ways of defending it, of hanging on to it. The

three defenses that we develop in later stages are blame placing, manipulation, and withdrawal.

2. *Problem Drinking.* As drinkers we lose our amateur standing and become alcohol artists in distress. We sneak drinks and hide our supply. In our defense against the "dry" world, we seek the support of alibis and excuses to explain much of our drinking behavior. We never assume the responsibility for our actions if we can shift the blame elsewhere. We develop a technique of blame placing and become leaners.

The tragedy of the blame-placing habit is that we cannot be responsible for either bad or good things that happen to us. We get depressed and anxious about our inadequacy. After blaming other people too long we lose our identity. We get anxious about our blame-placing habit, and then guilt really assails us.

It is clear that there is a physiological sensitivity that we have cultivated or that we have brought to the fore in our drinking pattern. This physiological X factor is something that can be included in the general tendency to be sensitive, anxious, and guilty.

3. *Defiant Drinking.* Now as schemers we turn to the art of "conning" and manipulating. "Conning" means to control or to be controlled. It is even more devastating, more tragic, than blame placing. We get into the habit of overexpectancy, controlling and manipulating people to get what we want. After awhile, when our expectations are not fulfilled, we get depressed and deflated. Controlling eventually leads to a state of depression.

In the need to control ourselves we become alcohol fighters. We alternate between drinking and abstinence. We try to limit our drinking to certain times, certain places. We demonstrate the use of control and finally, of course, we also feel the loss of it many times, many ways. We are in a chronic state of conflict, switching back and forth in our allegiance.

We often exhibit expansive behavior, appearing grandiose and overconfident about what we can do or plan to do. We are apt to develop "telephonitis," which is a kind of control over the behaviors of others, and it is certainly grandiose, especially when we inspect the phone bill at the end of the month. Of course, the reaction to this behavior is seen in our depressions, from which we suffer from time to time.

4. *Resigned Drinking*. We surrender when we become completely committed to drinking, resigned to the tyranny of our disorder. During this stage we are afraid of our drinking pattern but equally fearful of sobriety. So we try violently, painfully, to stay sober for long periods of time. Then these periods of abstinence, of course, are viciously broken by deep prolonged binges. We become periodic drinkers, even though our pattern before this may have been spasmodic and daily chronic. The lone drinking stage primarily illustrates the binge. It may include daily drinking, but we drink now more alone than socially with others.

On all sides we experience a breakdown of our alibis. People do not believe our stories any more; they are even suspicious of correct explanations that we may offer for our behavior. We find that we cannot even convince ourselves of the story that we want to relate to reduce our distress and fear.

This is the stage where we need others and then are alienated from them. We find ourselves afraid of life, suffering from a terrifying, nameless fear.

Being chronically afraid makes us unable to cope with anything unfamiliar. Therefore we withdraw and become self-sufficient loners. We experience deep loneliness that is not reduced by drinking. We may also suffer from physical disorders.

5. *Personal Decline.* In this stage we are inveterate drunks. All pleasure is gone. We suffer from a loss of tolerance and of our defenses. There is a complete loss of freedom, an utter dependence of the worst kind without knowing why.

Occasionally in delirium or in a deeply drunken state, there is a response, or so it seems, from the objects around us—sometimes ecstatic, more often dreadful. In the ecstatic state, we feel unity. In the dreadful state, we feel ugly conflict. Allen tells us about it:

I was exhausted, falling down drunk. I wandered off the highway into a quiet, secluded wood. I lay down and at once felt part of the warm, comfortable earth supporting me. I looked up at the trees swaying slightly around me. They seemed to say, "Yes, yes," over and over again. The feeling that swept through me was clear, joyous, peaceful. I was suddenly sober, light, and incredibly free.

More often, I have felt deep terror in the prospect of seeing a face so hideously contorted, so shakingly nameless, that I trembled in great agitation, sweating and gasping for release. In many nightmares, I awakened just a moment before the disintegrated face was about to show itself.

During personal decline we experience a vague, insistent religious longing. We feel obliged to review the whole meaning of our life, our relationship to others, to our community, to God or to the lack of God.

Our drinking problem has become a pattern of inhibition in contrast with sobriety, which is a creative effort. When we become aware of and accept the loss of our defenses, we can take the first step toward sobriety.

The Meaning of Our Drinking Problem

Malcolm Lowry, in *Under the Volcano,* neatly describes the plight of the alcoholic: "He was aware of a desire at once for complete glutted oblivion and for an innocent, youthful fling." The desire for oblivion and the urge to have a fling share common ground. Both are the longing for unity. The drunken coma is certainly not what the drinker originally intended. It is a blocked effort to feel joy in adventure. In the drinker's frustration, next best is oblivion, which falls far short of the original intention. But the alcoholic seeks oblivion because he wants unity, even at an insane price.

Along the way to the passout stage, the alcoholic feels the nostalgia for the good old days, the original urge for a fling. The original dream never dies. Neither does the alcoholic's inability to drink.

What was the real meaning of your original dream drinking? After the first year or so does it continue to do for you what it did at the start? Does it relax you, make you feel free, young, adventurous? If so, hang on to it. If it does not, hang on to the dream anyway.

If your alcoholism is like mine, the meaning is this: I drank to be free, and I lost my freedom. I drank to be adventurous, and I got boring and dull. I drank to be friendly, I wound up lonely. Drinking failed to do all that I first expected of it. It brought me the opposite of my original good intentions, leaving me frustrated, inhibited, depressed.

As a way of life, drinking is based on the philosophy of things, of having things. It represents the pleasure-power principle, and the logical outcome of that is addiction. If we believe that pleasure is the only thing in the world, there isn't anything better to do than to become addicted to alcohol, pills, or something else. Pain, of course, is part of the pleasure-power principle. Many people ignore that fact. Pain and pleasure are not opposed; they are like two sides of one coin. We cannot be pleased without taking into account that there is going to be a letdown, and the letdown is always painful.

Loss of Freedom

No one has to explain his drinking if he drinks in a socially acceptable fashion. A person is free to drink as long as he drinks responsibly without damage to himself or others.

The first sure sign of the loss of freedom as drinkers is our use of alibis. We do not turn to the use of excuses and explanations until we need their support to divert our critics.

Only the person who has lost his freedom to drink responsibly will turn to the use of supports—a pattern of blame placing. Only the person who has lost his discipline of living will turn to the use of controls—a pattern of manipulating or being manipulated. Only the person who has lost his capacity or desire to love will turn to techniques of self-reliance and withdrawal. All these losses occur in the alcoholic's way of life. But the first to go, the capacity to be free and easy, is the one most missed, the one most needed. Hence the thirst for freedom.

Loss of freedom, the first sure sign of alcoholism, can often occur long before any medical help is indicated. It can neither be treated by medicine nor overcome by controls. To try to *make* a person free is the surest way to make him unfree.

Each of us is responsible for the loss of freedom. The fact that we did not want it that way makes no difference. The fact that conditions in our lives, either within ourselves or in our social scene, weighed heavily in favor of our drinking does not change the truth. We are still responsible. I stress the word "intention" and avoid the word "motive." Intention encompasses the personal longing for freedom. By contrast, motive is part of the sickness-cure approach to alcoholism.

When I ask, "What did you intend to do last Tuesday when you got drunk" you feel more responsible for your behavior than if I should ask "What was the motive for your getting drunk last Tuesday?" The first question stresses faith in your freedom. The second gives you a chance to exercise the alibi, to escape the responsibility of your drinking. It belongs to a treatment method that could keep a therapist busy as long as his patient lived! The smart patient could unearth an endless variety of possible motives.

No amount of intervention or of confrontation will reach the patient at depth with any lasting worth if the patient has not been encouraged to believe in his own freedom, even when he is defensive and afraid.

Problem drinking is not primarily a sickness nor a moral problem. Although sickness and moral lapses may well occur, they do not constitute the main problem. When we accept the drinking pattern as an art, however defective, we have nothing to attack, criticize, or get rid of. We recognize the defect as a shortcoming—a well-intended act that simply fell short of a productive outcome.

Though it was the intention to be free by drinking, the capacity to feel free and easy somehow got lost in the drinking pattern. Respect that basic intention—to be free and easy and joyful and pursue it further. The relation of alcoholism to sobriety is the relation of the part to the whole.

The freedom lost in alcoholism can be found again, better than ever, in sobriety. We have to stop drinking and learn a new technique. Part of that technique we use in the recognition of why alcohol fails.

Why Alcohol Fails

Here are four practical reasons why alcohol fails to fulfill its early promise in the days of dream drinking:

1. The drinker gets the opposite of what he wants. Once free, adventurous, and amiable, he is now inhibited, imitative, frustrated, and lonely.

2. He increases his drinking to get the feeling he seeks, and with that comes an increase in tolerance—he needs more alcohol for less joy. He loses his freedom as he more deeply depends on the support of alibis. After a drinking spree, he experiences deeper distress. Pain exceeds pleasure and the feeling of release.

3. After loss of discipline, he needs patterns of control. He turns to will power or to modification techniques. Var-

ious measures, in the form of control, cannot manage the demonic world, the creative center of his being. Deep feelings are roused in intoxication that cannot be handled either by rational controls or by alcohol-induced techniques.

4. After loss of love, he tries to be self-sufficient by withdrawing from other people.

As stated before, alcohol is based on the philosophy of things. It stirs up within us the raw urges of what we are but it cannot discipline us. Based on the philosophy of things, alcohol is a "having." What we are requires contact with other human beings like ourselves. In deep alcoholism, we are withdrawn. In this state, alcohol no more fills the need to express ourselves, to realize our dreams, than food can make the overeater happy.

When sodden unity is prized above all the pain, fears, and sickness that precede and follow it, the drinker is addicted at depth, unable to use common sense to release him from his misery. He was at first addicted to a deep feeling of joy, of at-oneness, not primarily to alcohol. The way he wanted to feel was what mattered. This feeling faded, degenerated, as he grew addicted to alcohol. Still, he prizes this feeling in spite of the failure of alcohol in all other areas. This is the mystery of addiction. The problem is to inspire him with the hope of at-oneness in a sobriety program, where the dream has a chance to be realized.

Chapter 3

Hang On To What You Want

Attack Treatments

Before discussing attack treatments and why they fail, let us consider a few important terms. I equate ego with self, or human being. Human being is related to *person* as a part to the whole. Person is more than human being; it is a self who is free. Freedom arises from two or more people in a personal relationship where empathy flourishes. Empathy means knowing you, accepting you as though you were I and also as a completely "other" in his own right. Personal discipline is the exercise of empathy in the service of love, love of oneself as well as of others.

Attack treatments for alcoholism include will power, aversion treatments, behavior modification programs, and contract psychologies. For the most part, they are nonempathic. Their authoritarian battle cry is "Modify, cure, or control." Unlike empathy, which unifies, attack divides, putting one force into conflict with another. Such "cure" programs and all fears that accompany them are obstacles to feeling good. And they are obstacles to personal meaning.

The view that alcoholism is a sin gives rise to the moral model. The view that alcoholism is a medical problem gives rise to the sickness model. Both treatment models are based on the same philosophy—the value of control.

In the moral model, drinking is "bad" and abstinence is good. Self-control, or will power, will conquer the drinking problem. This moral model sets up a continuous battle between the "higher" and the "lower" self. Morally, you should not lose control. If you do, you surrender, you confess you are beaten, and you become penitent. Presumably, in the moral model you stop drinking for a reason opposite to the reason you first drank. You become good by ceasing to be "bad."

The moral model is completely ego-oriented, and an ego state is the natural home of an addiction. By an ego state I mean any experience, process, or act governed by self-will. Will power, for example, is an expression of self-will. It arises from an ego-oriented position. You, within your own skin, are determined to be abstinent by your own power. Will power is purpose without desire, which always ends in failure. Everybody who has ever tried it knows that it is worthless when you want to practice your habit in a way to make you feel good. It is painful, frustrating, depressing.

Aversion treatments, behavior modification programs, and contract psychologies shift the control out of self to the care of experts. Experts will do the job that you cannot do with your own self-control. Such attack treatments are as much ego-oriented as the moral model. The shift is simply from self to another "contractor"!

What is lacking in the attack exponents' approaches? All assume that the habit needs to be broken or controlled. Stressing the unpleasant, "bad," or fearful features of the problem, they use modification techniques in which the alcoholic finds himself uncomfortable, tense, or pained in the practice of his habit. He will either break or control his alcoholism, they reason, because he will stop wanting to behave as he used to behave.

Attack treatments ignore a basic truth about alcoholics. Even when they are in trouble, alcoholics have a sense of adventure. They will find ways to indulge their habit in the absence of controls and conditionings. They never forget their desire to feel good. Making them fearful of their habit by the use of unpleasant controls only builds their defenses against the controls. Offhand drinking, with all its trouble, is not as grim as controlled drinking or aversion treatments.

Why do alcoholics return, time and again, to their old habit after they have become addicted, bored, and lonely? They are in search of themselves, and they do not know a better way to relax, to achieve the unity they long to feel.

A program of freedom must offer the alcoholic the prospect of something he has always longed for. He can only stop drinking for the same good reason that he first drank, or for at least a similarly good reason. That reason stresses what he wants, not what is wrong with him.

In his sobriety or in his prospect of it, he still wants what he wanted in the dream stage of drinking. Because of that simple fact there is no need to break the habit. Neither is there any need to modify his sick behavior or to recondition his original intention. His original intention was the same as it is now—to feel good. The attack methods do less than nothing on that score.

Even if the attack-control techniques make an alcoholic abstinent for a time, the value of that abstinence is in great doubt. Attack techniques are fear models that grossly neglect man's need to be resourcefully free. Exponents of the fear models fail to realize that simply the removal of pain and the negative relief of pleasure that results from it are not enough to guarantee sobriety. They fail to see that the drinker's desire to be free, the first among the elusive qualities of feeling good, is more important than pleasure and the absence of pain. Actually, pleasure and "feeling no pain" are important features of the disorder in its problem form. To induce, by controls, a desire to overprize comfort and the absence of pain is actually to reinforce the fearful features of the active drinking routine!

The attack techniques are all double-rutted approaches —spirit-flesh, good-evil, mind-body, health-sickness, maturity-immaturity. The common divisive tool is subject-object. This is the logical technique in all efforts that seek control, either self-control or scientific control.

Drinking begins as an art of feeling good. So, too, sobriety is an art of feeling good. What we seek is harmony, not opposition. There is so such thing as a clean break. We carry our alcoholism right into our sobriety. We could not well control our drinking in our drinking pattern. We cannot well control our drinking in our sobriety. We do not fight this incapacity. We accept it.

To observe the contrast between the attack modalities and the meaning model that I propose, let us look at the problem in terms of a continuous dynamic flow.

1. Drinking begins. Here there is devotion to the desire to feel good.

2. Routine sets in. When a drinking session is initiated, it is often (not always, but often) difficult to discontinue it.

This practice often leads to a sick reaction—the hangover, organic and systemic disorders, or behavioral problems such as anxiety, depression, and withdrawal.

In spite of all trouble, the drinker seeks the unity of deep drunkenness, sodden at-oneness. The price he pays is high, but he seeks this condition, often in danger of death. This unity is prized above the normal run of pleasure and the prevalence of pain. The drinker is aware of joy and he desires to avoid pain, but he will forfeit joy and assume pain for the sake of that mysterious need to "get it all together," if only in the sodden unity of deep intoxication.

3. The unity of a deep addictive state is not the opposite of sobriety because a sober person wants integrity as deeply as the sick alcoholic. Of course, a sober man will want a more creatively conceived unity than the one he knew in drunkenness.

We derive the meaning model from the dynamics of addiction. This meaning model is neither mental-health oriented nor medically oriented. And it is certainly not moral oriented. I do not seek to locate symptoms of ill health in a medico-psychological critique and then say that alcoholism is only a symptom. In 1960 I made that clear in *Thirst for Freedom,* when I stressed that alcoholism is a disorder in its own right. I stressed even more the need to cultivate the art of sobriety beyond the treatment of our distress.

It is, of course, important to become well in order to feel good. Medical science can help here on the physical level as well as at the level of deep sickness, where a patient is incapable of thinking for himself. In cases of deep sickness, the patient might die without such emergency treatment. However, such emergency care at best is only provisional. It should not be made a policy of full treatment.

It should be remembered that alcoholics have deep personal problems, just as other people do. But, as a class, alcoholics have no more deeply sick people than any other class. Therefore there is no need to belabor all their quirks and defects. What is more significant is to be on the lookout for signs of the leaner, schemer, or loner. After all, those signs are not so much symptoms of disease as they are signs of being human.

Alcoholism as a Self-Design

In the meaning model, you move from the drinking pattern, a self-design, into sobriety, a personal design, in a sequential flow—not by opposing alcoholism and sobriety. In the meaning model, the design is grounded in the reason both for drinking and sobriety—to feel good, to quench personal thirst.

As an alcoholic, your design begins in a life of having, a self-design. All self-designs fail because they lose their purpose. The purpose is lost to the desire that the purpose used to discipline. The desire, then, with the purpose lost, brings the opposite of what was first wanted.

Drinking loses the purpose of feeling good. The desire to drink, however, continues after you fail to feel good the way you used to. You continue to destroy yourself until you extend your design for living from self-concern to the richer context of personal meaning.

How can you move from a self-design to a personal design? Begin with this questionnaire:

1. Do you feel you are in trouble?

2. Have you lost your freedom to drink as you once did, easy and relaxed?

3. Do you have to control your drinking?

4. Do you withdraw and drink alone? Do you want to be self-sufficient?

5. Can you accept the view that your habit is the reason why you drank? The habit is the personal thirst to feel good.

If the answer is "yes" to three of these five questions, you can begin in a simple way.

Respect Your Personal Thirst

Your habit was developing before you got into trouble with alcohol. Before your drinking problem, you had acquired the habit of feeling good, the habit of wanting to be freely and easily yourself. You were thirsty even before you got drunk. That personal thirst is the real habit, the reason why you drink. Drinking was not the reason for your personal habit. You do not get the habit from your drinking; you get the drinking from your habit. And it is a thirst you cannot quench with alcohol—"One drink is too many and a thousand not enough."

So hang on to what you want! Respect that personal thirst to feel good, to be free and easy, wanting fun and companionship. Don't be ashamed of the trouble it has brought you. Every sensitive person is at some time in deep distress. But don't be proud of your capacity for control, even if you still use it successfully. Control, successful or not, is the problem. It takes over after you have lost your freedom.

If you have given up control, you are on the right path. That, of course, does not mean that you can go on drinking. To continue, after control fails, is to fight alcohol. The only way to abandon control is to stop drinking. In abstinence, in good will, there is no need for control at all. Your control is given over to discipline, or the pursuit of what you want outside of alcohol. It is always practiced in concert with others to help achieve what you want.

The Thirst for Freedom

The desire to stop drinking can only endure when it becomes the desire to be free. The thirst for freedom can only be quenched in the discipline of fellowship where the purpose, sobriety, is achieved day by day.

Though early drinking and sobriety have basic ideals in common, the difference between their pursuit in drinking and in sobriety should be carefully noted. As a drinker, you wanted to feel good, pleased, in order to feel free, adventurous, loving. As a sober person, the priority of wants is reversed: you first want to be free in order to feel good.

Instead of submitting now to drinking, now to abstinence, you recognize the entire problem for what it is, uncontrollable. And you see yourself for what you are, unmanageable, but all together, not as a divided self using a control technique. Instead of surrender to a master, a tyrant, or a superior power of any kind, you become acquainted with others as an equal, a fellow sufferer, in fellowship.

The capacity to become an agent, a free human being, is what it means to be a person. As an agent you become more free as you show more concern for a project other than yourself or for yourself. This does not mean that you neglect yourself. On the contrary, you best serve yourself as a free agent when you devote most of your interest to another person, place, or thing.

Human know-how is concerned with money, power,

and sex—wanting to have, to get, to control. Personal know-how is concerned with wanting to be and to become the person you potentially are.

Personal know-how begins with learning to be free. There is no way you can be free without other people. Your need for others is a personal want, above all human wants. You need their friendship, their insight, into your faults and shortcomings. With them you can learn to be free, creative, and loving.

Through personal know-how you get in touch with your real personal thirst, to feel good. Then you recognize that you drifted into haphazard routines in your drinking pattern. Here you observed loss of freedom, loss of discipline, loss of love. Awareness of these losses is expressed in your personal thirst to know them again.

As a problem drinker nothing impresses you as much as recognition of your loss of freedom. Next is the loss of your enjoyment when you lose discipline. Third is the loss of fellowship when you feel obliged to withdraw. You do not much care about loss of support, of control, of ego; they were painful anyway. What you really miss is being care-free, adventurous, friendly. That is what you want again.

Chapter 4

From Alcoholism To Sobriety

Freedom Symbols in the Drinking Pattern

The adventure from drinking to freedom is an act of enrichment, deeper meaning. It is a discovery of something more, not a denial of what you are or have been. It is a creative act from inhibition to release, from half person to whole person, from sign to symbol. To move from sign to symbol reveals the capacity to act, not simply to react.

From having to being, from quantity to quality, from control to discipline, from ego to person, from crackup to integrity—in all these transitions there is no fight, no denial, no surrender. There is simply the joyous insight that it is better to be fully than partially alive, better to be integrated than divided. Whatever you have been, whatever you have valued, is carried right into your sobriety. You are human and remain so when you become a person. It is just that being a person becomes more important than being human.

Each stage of alcoholism is the thirst for something more. And each stage of the drinking pattern permeates each corresponding stage of the sobriety pattern.

The five stages of the drinking pattern, discussed in

Chapter 2, merge into the five steps of freedom. As you trace the meaning of your drinking, these ten steps, as shown in Table 2, are an exercise in the skill of recognition.

Observe that addiction and freedom are not opposed. The exemplary ideal, freedom, is conditioned by slavery. Instead of attack or control, there is acceptance and creative effort.

From the first to the last you are not told precisely how to behave. To be instructed in the details of action would be a violation of freedom and a blocking of creative effort. You are only given the conditions of resourceful behavior. As in the Beatitudes, you are consoled by the promise that to be defective is to be "blessed," well prepared for the joyous adventure of vigorous living.

The crisis that follows the long chronic conflict of the alcoholic, or any other habitué for that matter, is not that of a defeated person who is about to surrender something. Rather, it is that of a musician who is getting together the discordant elements of his conflict into a resourceful ongoing unity. He creates harmony where there was once discord. It is a harmony of all that he is, not a rejection of part of him in abject defeat.

You do not have to be musically talented in order to appreciate and apply the conditions of music. Most people, in the daily pursuit of joyous living, seek harmony, beauty of form, and good timing.

From Having to Being

As an alcoholic you are addicted to having. And you live in a society addicted to having, fulfilling human wants of money, power, and sex. People who derive

Table 2

FROM ALCOHOLISM TO FREEDOM

Five Steps of Alcoholism

Stage	Characteristics	Addiction Signs
1. dream drinking (amateur alcohol artist)	free and easy, adventurous, friendly	dramatic change of feeling sought
2. problem drinking (alcohol artist in distress)	blackouts	need and use of support (alibis)
3. defiant drinking (alcohol fighter)	abstinence, binges	need and use of control
4. resigned drinking (the lush)	physical disorders, loneliness	nameless fears, collapse of defenses, need and use of self-sufficiency
5. personal decline (inveterate drunk)	loss of tolerance	loss of defenses—support, control, self-sufficiency

Five Steps of Freedom

Stage	Freedom Symbols
6. awareness of loss of defenses	from sign to symbol
7. loss of support enables you to make real contact with others	contact, personableness activity
8. loss of control enables you to recognize the urge to be creative	hopefulness, compassion, practicality
9. loss of self-sufficiency enables you to become acquainted	loving, peace-making, imaginative nature
10. in the good disposition where empathy arises, the free alcoholic finds the courage to be himself	

their meaning of life from what they own are governed by the possession principle. Their lives are dominated by the quantity dogma, the belief that everything can be counted, measured, controlled. How do we foster a life of being in a society largely committed to the philosophy of things?

The pleasure-power principle that governs alcoholics represents an effort to break away from a poorly understood dependence. In an effort to be free, the alcoholic turns to drinking. The struggle for freedom is understandable and commendable, but the technique is faulty. As stated earlier, having brings problems of being "had." And that is what happens to the alcoholic when he delivers himself into the power of alcohol.

The way from having to being begins with acceptance, which is founded in good will. You begin with acceptance of yourself, particularly of your defects. You accept others like yourself, suffering from the same disorder. To be is to be well disposed toward yourself and others.

Personal know-how is based on good will—what you want that is best for you and for others. At the start you have to accept your defects—the habits of leaning, scheming, and withdrawing. These you can put into the history of your life simply by discussing them and by discovering that they are self-techniques, of little use to you as a person. To be yourself means to become free, adventurous, and companionable. Although these are the same goals of your early drinking days, now there is a vast change in attitude. That change is from fear for self to acceptance of self and others in good will.

Conflicts such as good vs. evil, spirit vs. flesh, mind vs. matter, sober vs. drunk come from efforts to fight, dominate, or control yourself. For example, the "spirit," or will power, decides what the "flesh" can or cannot do. However, will power is only a resolution of a part person. Therefore, the spirit is not qualified to direct a resolution of staying sober because the whole person is needed to initiate and develop the practice of sobriety. Only in unified thinking, in your desires as a whole person, can you do what you decide to do.

That is why you decide to accept what you find and do what you can, creatively, to live a fuller life, not by control but by discipline. The way from having to being is not an abandonment of having. Rather, it is to realize that having is secondary to being.

The way to being is to feel the importance of *person time*—real time as you experience it in the creative center of your life. Time as you feel it is different from the time upon which you impose measures, like your watch. Your watch is spatialized time, but your inner tempo is what I call *real time*. When you say "I had a good time," you refer to the quality of an incident, not to its measure. In this sense, you cannot divide time nor can you measure it as you measure time on a clock.

The same is true of action. While in the act itself you neither measure nor control. There is no pleasure measure in real time as there was when you drank, pouring into a glass the amount you needed for a drug-powered "high." The materialistic technique in drinking was not nearly capable of giving you freedom, still it gave promise of it in a minute way. Nothing else could explain why you went on drinking, in great misery, except the occasional flash of that inner feeling of free time—indivisible, uncontrollable, unified.

Ordinary measures do not touch that inner life, the creative personal center of time and action and feeling. No wonder A.A. says "A day at a time." There is great depth in that slogan as well as in the advice "Don't overdo." "A day at a time" is all you can live in the life of being free, adventurous, and loving.

From Quantity to Quality

The acting "I"—the source of personal know-how—is fluid and dynamic, like the real time in which it exists. All efforts to portray the "I" by control, as in ego-oriented theories, leave out what is most important about the "I" in time—its flow, its unity, its duration.

It is the same with the use of controls in the study of intoxication. Most professional studies of alcoholism omit what we really want to know. They are discussions about and around drinking. None are about drinking itself. Such studies ignore what is most meaningful about being drunk —the quality of intoxication.

A symbolism, a model, is needed that will do justice to the quality of intoxication and therefore to the quality of sobriety. In drunkenness are exciting clues of what you will pursue in sobriety.

Attack-control techniques are "know-that" approaches, which represent a fence separating you from what is known. By contrast, know-how is a flow into what you want to know, an action, dynamic, moving, taking you to the heart of the matter. Know-how, instead of "know-that," is a gateway to knowledge of quality.

Personal know-how is an art. It is more like music than anything else. It aims at the balance of all senses. It is the capacity to express what your feelings are really like.

Practiced in fellowship, it exhibits rhythm, a sense of form in spontaneous give and take.

Bars and clubs well know the value of music in their business. Alcoholics grope for that unity, that at-oneness, in their distaste for the unanonymous world, where there is more conflict, more separateness, than harmony and communion.

Time and space come together in music as in no other art. The same can be said of content and form. The sound of music I can feel in two ways at once. I can feel the space between the notes, between the chords, and I can feel the time they take in the context of the tune. But as I listen or play, I need not be aware of the two separate existences. I feel unity. The separation is only felt in discussion or reflection. The sound of you, in touch with me as a friend, is much the same.

Music conveys feelings that language cannot express. So, too, in ordinary discourse are nuances and details of the way we feel that words cannot convey.

As persons, we are related to one another as notes to a chord, as chords to a tune. In a personal context, we become as one, yet each of us is distinctly himself.

We feel an "intention" in a tune—a theme with an opening, a bridge, a return to the opening in the finish. The pattern is similar to the intention, technique, and practice in personal know-how.

In A.A. groups the personal story has become a tradition. What is there about "the story" that persists as a main feature of the A.A. program? There are many views about its value—catharsis, "getting it off your chest," a sharing of experiences, strength and hope, making your inventory, making amends, carrying the message. There are more opinions than can be counted. But a few things are clear. We make contact with the speaker, we recognize a lot of what he says, and we get better acquainted with our problem and with him. Personal know-how is an action and it is musical, whatever else we may call it.

In a way I do not yet fully understand music figures centrally in the adventure of learning to be ourselves, through and beyond addiction. In many ways the meaning model resembles the meaning of music in the search for the start, middle, and finish of any experience, the use of repetition, the respect for duration and endurance, the unity of life in melody, harmony, and good timing—disciplined yet free, imitative yet creative, "out there" yet intimate.

Quality in personally felt time is being. I cannot know this in you except by empathic intuition—my belief that you experience life in a way similar to me. I can feel your intoxication by recalling my own, then by comparing notes with you in a dialogue of good will. To do this is to engage in personal know-how. We do better to compare our feelings than our theories. I can savor the quality of your feelings not by submitting you to controls but by reporting my feelings to you and inviting your response.

Bergson used a tune to illustrate what he meant by pure duration, pure time. Our meaning, he said, is "the continuous melody of inner life."

Duration, personally felt time, is essentially musical. Spoken words in personal dialogue, when you and I are feeling our way into meaning, along with pauses, form a melodic continuity, a personal whole. A tune has the unity of a progressive act; it is not a thing.

As we go from note to note, we build a form that we cannot reduce to a succession of separate hearings. We carry the theme to a finish, a completed whole. As we do, we feel a sense of anticipation, as though we already knew that what we hear this moment is not complete by itself, that we have yet to feel richer unity. Listening is a kind of mysterious recognition.

Our anonymous past, from our creative center, emerges from inner depths and takes form in our feeling, colored by our personal history. What we feel is qualitative. It comes from a source ancient in our personal history, long before we were born, from I know not where. It is anonymous.

To exchange stories coming from the heart is to feel the quality of life that the quantity dogma cannot illumine. The quantity dogma gives us time only as known in space. Any view of alcoholism that stresses only alcohol is based on the quantity dogma.

For example, behavior controllers stress the drinking routine. Our view of alcoholism stresses reason and intention, as well as drinking. The real creative urge is in the intention, whose source is in free time, real duration. It is time as we personally feel it, not measured or controlled. We can choose to select another technique —we do not have to drink because tomorrow is a new day and need not be like today if we decide to act differently. A choice is available to us from the inside, where we live, but not possible to us in terms of the quantity dogma.

In the scientific "know-that" approach to alcoholism the habit comes first, intention second. In other words, habit causes the intention. In the personal know-how approach, intention initiates and forms the early habit. The intention comes first and matters most. It can therefore discipline the direction of the habit. It antici- pates unity.

The cause of trouble in alcoholism is not the intention —everybody means well—but the technique. We have only to intend a different technique and we extend the scope of the habit into an art that achieves what we in- tend. The habit is then fulfilled, no longer inhibited by a faulty technique.

I share much with you in the content of what I want, what I intend to be. But the inner personal nature of what I intend is unique to me, as your intention is unique to you. The intentions spring from deep sources within the personal creative center of each of us. Intention is an experience of quality, not ever to be quantified.

People who are governed by the possession principle, dominated by the quantity dogma, are known as leaners. They reveal an anxious need for support, both material and personal. Their fear of blame leads to blame placing. After loss of support, they thirst to be free; they thirst for that quality of being that delivers them from being "had." With the discovery of quality, they become free persons, they move from having to being. As leaners, they were anxious and guilty. As free beings, they become persona- ble and active.

The main clue to the change is found in the discovery that we are our intentions. No one else can choose for us. In our intentions is found the quality we seek, if we are sure that our intentions center on being free.

From Control to Discipline

Underlying the quantity dogma and the possession principle is the urge to control or exploit. That is an urge that may be applied to things but not to people. The demons, the urges deep within us that came into our life from ancient history, cannot be controlled or exploited. However, they can be aggravated and disturbed in all control efforts.

With the philosophy of things as his creed, the alcoholic regards his deep inner personal life like everything else in the unanonymous, "square," world. That creative personal center is to be exploited, manipulated, controlled. That is all the alcoholic knows—his control devices.

He suspects there is deep mystery in desire, in the play of feelings he cannot easily understand, but he conceals his uneasy suspicion and at the same time thirsts for the submerged excitement.

In a state of deep addiction the truth comes out. What he thought he could control now controls his entire life. Control is the main problem of every addict—the need for it, the use of it, the fear of the loss of it.

What the alcoholic encounters is the demonic world, that deep creative personal center of his life. It is stronger than any conscious control, beyond all the "cons" and angles of his scheming behavior.

All addicts fear the loss of freedom. They cannot bear to believe that they have lost their grip. Once they used to drink for the fun of it. Now they seek control. No matter how much they want to contact and let loose their unruly world, they do not want the inner center of their life to become part of their sober behavior. There is real fear here. They want to feel what they deeply are. They want to express their selves at depth. But they can only feel and express their "demons" armed with a lame excuse: "I had a ball last night, but of course you know I was stoned out of my mind."

If alcoholics could understand their problem as an effort to express themselves creatively, they would not seek alibis for behavior. Rather, they would try to find a discipline that enables them to accept themselves and to express what they are, not to reject it in shame. However, if they regard their problem as a moral lapse, they become defensive and self-righteous. If they regard alcoholism as only a medical problem, they become too resigned. Best of all is to regard addiction as a problem of art.

Failure to see the problem as an art leads to defiance and the use of will power, which are ego-bound approaches. Then the schemer emerges with his need for control or manipulative devices and alibis. Locked-in defenses result in depression. If the alcoholic responds effectively to the thirst for form and harmony, he is brought to discipline rather than control. The challenge is to move from control to discipline, from science and morality to art and personal know-how.

In all my studies since *Thirst for Freedom* I have stressed the art of sobriety as practiced in the principles of personal know-how. Sobriety is the concern of a way of life. This involves philosophy, the study of personal meaning and ways to practice it. Such practice will involve good health and competent psychological insight. But at depth it will involve much more—the elusive art of feeling good.

Many people talk about physical factors in alcoholism,

and scientific research proceeds space along those lines. However, I believe that the explanation, when it is more clear, more in context with everything involved, will reveal a complex personal process rather than a strictly biological entity.

In coping with the sick components of alcoholism, therapists need all the help they can get from medical colleagues. Where personal trouble adds a complication to the disorder, the assistance of behavior consultants is required.

But here I am talking primarily about the prospect of feeling good and how to achieve that feeling. In the attack-control methods, the prospect of feeling good is bleak and fruitless. These methods fail for the same reason that drinking failed. Like drinking, they are forms of having. They do not and cannot make us feel good because they are fear-ridden, just as alcoholism, late in addiction, is a fearful indulgence.

The way to freedom is through acceptance and being. We accept our habit; we do not break it. We seek to be rather than to have. Having divides and destroys, while being integrates.

We can distinguish between control and discipline in a number of ways:

Control	*Discipline*
selfish, an act of defiance	personal, involving others
an act of fear	an act of love
having and being "had"	being
essence of science	essence of art
dualistic (subject outside of object)	unitary (free within the problem)

Control and discipline are not opposed. Only a problem in human behavior arises when control is sought to the exclusion of discipline.

The alcoholic reveals an impaired capacity to love: with a habitual dependence on alcohol, people, and feelings of his own he does not understand. The way out is through discipline of love by means of empathy.

Productive questions to ask ourselves are: how free am I? how creative? how loving? What are the techniques of freedom, art, and love? They are contact, recognition, and acquaintance in fellowship. These give us intention, technique, and practice in personal discipline. Rather than inhibiting or controlling our creative personal strivings, we use discipline to express them.

As schemers, depressed and despairing, we graduate from control to discipline, where as creative beings we become hopeful and practical.

From Ego to Person

Eventually the ego-bound alcoholic retreats into a self-sufficient shell. He is false in his loneliness, without the contact that nourishes his meaning. In withdrawal, he lives in a vacuum—not in the past, not in the future, and certainly not in the present. Real time stands still. Only the ticking of a clock, monotonous, boring, measures out his hours. That real personal time, inside, where he feels free and integrated, is empty. Nothing meaningful happens, time evaporates, freedom disappears when, in isolation, he is wrapped up in himself and out of touch with others. Alone, he is without meaning. As a loner, he is "had," fearful, static. He thirsts for love.

To find, to feel, love, he must get in touch with others. In the search for meaning he discovers nothing in himself, by himself. Alone, he loses his sense of real time because he is out of action. To act again, to be free again, he must contact another human being like himself. In this move he emerges from the bound ego into the life of a person.

He finds truth in fellowship, he finds his meaning through another. No matter how much he owns, he cannot enjoy it if he has no meaning, no being. He can only enjoy what he has by being himself, and he can only be himself through another person or persons.

As a person, he becomes committed and imaginative. He becomes free when his sense of real time is restored. He feels his identity as he endures life, from day to day, with a sense of meaningful continuity, recognizing, putting together features of his life that used to be fragmented, without purpose or design. But he can also anticipate the unknown in the sense of ongoing adventure in the restoration of real personal time. Time no longer stands still. Life no longer bores. He is alive again in the real time of his inner person. He is free and adventurous once more and learning how to love.

Real time is felt personally only when, at comparative rest, we observe the movement of something outside ourselves. We cannot sense this movement in time if we are bound egos, closed up within ourselves. What happens to each of us, by ourselves, with our vision withdrawn, dwelling only on ourselves, is just a series of fragmented thoughts and feelings, without duration, without continuity. In this prison we cannot be free because we cannot honestly choose to move or change.

The paradox is this: to feel genuine inner personal time,

a sense of continuity or endurance, we have to be aware of the world outside ourselves—the world of people in action, not of things, clocks, watches, and calendars. We find meaning to the degree that we are aware of and in touch with others. This contact involves us in the skill of recognition and in the practice of fellowship. We become a person in fellowship and find our truth and meaning there.

From Crackup to Integrity

If the drinker stays with his problem long enough, he will suffer collapse in a crackup. Then all pleasure is gone. His dream is in shreds. Impotent, physically depleted, he has no capacity to make decisions of his own. He finds it hard to concentrate and make sense of anything. He shows an utter dependence of the worst kind on his fears and his need for alcohol. He experiences a vague insistent urge to find some meaning at depth. His inner creative center is all but gone, but a shred remains. In that shred there is a desperate longing to be integrated once more, and in the integrity to find some meaning for being alive.

Scott Fitzgerald, in his story "The Crack-Up," describes the alcoholic's tragic decline. It is an account of withdrawal. "I had a strong sudden instinct that I must be alone . . . and so arranged a certain insulation from ordinary cares." He thought that he had to make a clean break to survive. That was his ruin. Self-contained people seek to make a clean break. But there is really no way to cut other people and part of ourselves out of our meaning. To fight, to forget, to depart, or to withdraw from any side of ourselves is to invite ruin.

The way to integrity is not found in a break from any part of our lives but in creating a harmony among all the parts that belong to each of us. We accept even our addiction and go on thirsting. We accept others whom we need in the adventure of becoming a person.

The Meaning Model

The meaning model includes the sickness component; for alcoholism is a sickness, though much more than that. It includes the psychological and social components, for alcoholism certainly involves behavior defects in the individual and in the context of his social scene.

However, most important, alcoholism is a personal problem. This means that the capacity to be free, creative, and loving is impaired. The capacity to be a person, at depth, is an experience transcending good health and good psychosocial conditions. To be a person is both practical and mysterious. It is practical because no human being can be truly happy if he does not strive for more than money, power, and sex. It is practical to cultivate the technique of personal know-how simply to be yourself, to be myself. To be a person is mysterious because no one can prescribe what you or I need to be free, adventurous, and friendly. As with you, "It begins with me," it begins with my intentions. The fact that so much of what I feel is intentional, inside me, adventurous, never knowing precisely what in my freedom I may do, what or whom I may love—all this makes the personal mysterious.

The whole aim of personal know-how is to quench personal thirst. The acting "I," that creative personal center, is impossible to define. However, it can be felt in personal thirst, in various forms of longing.

The thirst to break out of controls that restrict and confine us is the thirst for freedom. The thirst for form, adventure, and joy is the thirst for beauty. The thirst for truth is the thirst for love, found in fellowship. The thirst for meaning is a personal thirst, the sum of the others and even more in the longing for personal identity and for the unknown, the realm of the anonymous. It is the desire to feel good, in the fullness of being.

If you are a "coach" or a therapist you do well to respect these forms of thirst, ahead of what you and an alcoholic say to one another. What you say is as bound to controls as what he says. What you do and how you feel are as important in you as in the alcoholic.

The acting "I" within the alcoholic may well be feeling very different from what he says to the therapist. The therapist, too, may be expressing thoughts at variance with his true feeling.

If sobriety is an art, we the "coaches" must show the alcoholic. How do we quench our thirst for freedom? Are we free? How do we quench our thirst for love? Are we loveworthy? How do we quench our thirst for meaning? Can the alcoholic recognize something meaningful, joyful, exciting in our quest for the worth of life? Can we be ourselves, truly ourselves, with him?

We should not make the alcoholic do anything that he does not choose to do. He has to start sometime to exercise his own freedom. The best we can do is to show him where we are.

The demonstration of ourselves as free alcoholics will foster his desire to become sober more effectively than any use of words, any use of pressure. The responsibility of the free alcoholic is great. What I as a free alcoholic communicate to my fellow alcoholic cannot be any better than I truly am, not more free, not more creative, not more loving than I can show him in what I do.

With the meaning model we do not break the habit of addiction—we fulfill it in sobriety. The relation of addiction to sobriety is the relation of the part to the whole. Sobriety is really an enjoyable diversion, not a cure, not a treatment, not a Sunday school lesson. Diversion fits better into the art of living than into medicine or morality. After all, drinkers drank for diversion. Why not be sober for the same reason?

The meaning model, as charted in separate stages, is a logical performance. In action, what happens and what is intended occur in a fluid, dynamic way, not in the orderly sequence shown in Table 3 on page 52. For example, we do not experience quantity becoming quality, control becoming discipline, ego becoming person, crackup becoming integrity, one neatly after the other. The insight that these are forms of the transition from having to being may well come anywhere in the process, even during or after crackup. The shock of recognition depends largely on the skills of the "coach."

The five features of sobriety—first being and then explicit forms of being (quality, discipline, personhood, and integrity)—all flow in a natural sequence from alcoholism into a quenching of personal thirst. The dynamics of design follow the reason common to drinking and sobriety, to feel good.

If, as an alcoholic, you can believe that you were thirsty before you drank, that drinking only deepened your craving, then you believe that your personal thirst is more important than all the trouble you had when you drank.

Table 3

THE MEANING MODEL

Self-Design of Alcoholism	*Personal Design of Sobriety*
INTENTION— to feel good	INTENTION— to feel good
HAVING— the half world of alcoholism, where you pursue pleasure through having drinks	BEING— the whole free world of sobriety, where you use personal know-how to realize the best of yourself
QUANTITY— governed by the possession principle and quantity dogma, you become a leaner; your use of support (alibis) indicates your loss of freedom	QUALITY— through contact you realize intention of being; the quality of freedom is felt in contact with others in similar trouble
CONTROL— in your ego-bound life, you become a schemer; your use of control reflects the loss of discipline	DISCIPLINE— through recognition you become adventurous, creative, and loving
EGO— in an ego retreat you become a self-sufficient loner; your withdrawal reflects a loss of love	PERSON— through acquaintance you learn to accept yourself, others, and your disorder; you experience time personally felt
CRACKUP— fearful, sick, and "had," you suffer a loss of devotion, of concentration, of purpose	INTEGRITY— you get it all together and you learn how to feel good enduringly
OUTCOME— personal thirst persists	OUTCOME— personal thirst quenched

You still thirst for freedom, beauty of life, love of friends. That thirst to feel good is the basic issue, not a reminder of how "sick" you are or how you fail to confront your problem.

In the meaning model we seek to identify loss of freedom, of discipline, of love. The thirst for these ideals
takes us directly to the art of personal know-how, which
is discussed at length in Chapter 7. Steps along the way
—from loss to thirst—are an exciting exercise in recognition.

Chapter 5

The Anonymous World

The A.A. Program

Freedom, adventure, and love flourish best in the anonymous world, not in the unanonymous world of quantity. In the Alcoholics Anonymous program, you can move from conflict and inhibition to free and joyous productive effort. The program is a transition from a life of having to a life of being.

The twelve steps and twelve traditions of A.A. give you the why, what, and how of sobriety. Why be sober? Simply to be more free, adventurous, and loving than you wanted to be when you first drank. What is sobriety? It is a fellowship of men and women who share their experience, strength, and hope to find release from their alcoholic trouble and help others do the same. Beyond release from their problem lies the learning and the joy that real sobriety can bring. How be sober? The way is anonymous, informal, spontaneous, joyful, and mysterious.

First must come the acceptance of alcoholism. Then all the rest of the program is designed to liberate you for richer action than you ever knew as an alcoholic. You are introduced to the quality of sober living. In a life of quantity the question is always "How much?" In a life of quality the question always is "How meaningful?" To go beyond alcohol and everything measurable and controllable is to turn from quantity to quality, from measure to freedom.

The A.A. program may be understood in terms of action, art, and personal mystery. These lead from various forms of the crackup to integrity, at-oneness. The action is the twelve steps, the art or informal technique is the twelve traditions, the personal mystery is the whole program. Integrity is gradually felt in the at-oneness achieved through the "recap" steps (10, 11, 12) and the slogans and prayers that integrate and guide the action and the technique.

The Twelve Steps

The twelve steps are a series of actions taken toward coping with your problem and becoming a person. Each step leads to, merges with, and supports the other steps as well as the twelve traditions (see pages 61–66).

Step 1: We admitted we were powerless over alcohol— that our lives had become unmanageable. This admission of total incapacity over alcohol and all aspects of life is taken in an anonymous fashion. The step uses "we," not you, not I. This "we" is the same as saying "I am one of a group that I identify as we."

It is a movement from "I can't be free alone" to "I can be free within limits among fellow alcoholics who admit they cannot drink and cannot manage or control their lives." It is a movement from loss of support to contact. You no longer lean on the old unsteady props, excuses, and people who used to shore you up. Instead, in contact, you share experience, strength, and hope in the pursuit of your common welfare.

Step 2: Came to believe that a Power greater than our-

selves could restore us to sanity. Realizing that you are completely powerless, you gradually came to believe in a greater power. There is no problem about the spiritual angle. If you cannot overcome alcoholism alone, and no one else can, and you see that fellow members are all sober, then you come to believe in a power greater than any of you.

The second step is a movement from loss of control to recognition. What you come to believe turns out to be something everyone can share, no matter how each of you differ in your personal views of the greater power. After many years' experience, the common belief is faith in the group conscience, a loving concern, not a control, not a human authority. The loving concern is the discipline A.A. members develop in their devotion to sobriety. For sobriety is an act of love, and so is the discipline that expresses it.

Step 3: Made a decision to turn our will and our lives over to the care of God as we understand Him. This third step gives you the personal right to understand God and the meaning of your life in your own way, without pre-scriptions, restrictions, inhibitions. It is a move from ego to person, from self-concern to a desire that can flourish only in acquaintance with others like yourself.

In Step 3 you made a decision. This capacity of choice, this act of freedom, comes from Steps 1 and 2. Unfree people cannot make sound decisions. As you became anonymous in Steps 1 and 2, you stopped fighting. When you forfeit your self-sufficiency, your human will, in Step 3, you are well inside the experience of anonymity where you will find the free, real person who is you.

How do you become free and real? The grace of God

you can interpret as the loss of the desire to drink and the loss of fear. The grace of God comes to your aid in helping you make a decision. The turning over of "our will and our lives" is a gesture of good will toward fellow alcoholics. The two actions that make you a free, real person come from anonymous sources: (1) God who helped you make the decision and (2) the good will toward the group who helped you understand.

Strange it is that what makes you a real person in your own right comes from outside of you and outside of any other person. It is something that you give to others in love. This reminds us, of course, that all addictions are love disorders and that the remedy for them can be nothing else but love.

The miracle, the value, and the beauty of Alcoholics Anonymous spring from the third step of the twelve-step program. This third step includes Steps 1 and 2 and anticipates 4 through 12. It also anticipates the twelve traditions.

The miracle of A.A. is this—you hit bottom so definitely that you find yourself without choice. The only choice you have is to stop drinking. So you relax quietly in the decision you make when you stop fighting. This is the principle "Don't fight evil." When you make this admission and recognize this condition, you begin to experience the miracle. In the recognition of utter helplessness and the decision to stop fighting you begin to see the light. "Don't fight evil" requires the acceptance of three losses—of support, of control, of self-sufficiency. These three losses correspond to the actions that you take respectively in the first three steps.

The beauty of Step 3 is in the phrase "as we understand

Him." In this experience, in this feeling of God as you understand Him, anonymity completes itself. The personal meaning is the source of insight into God, both within you and beyond. Within you, because you can understand Him only as He reveals Himself to you. Beyond, because in order to be God, to be beyond your control and knowing, He has to be *other*—He has to be distinctly other. You can only know Him as other if He is first at one with you. As you "understand Him" must refer to your highest ideals, your deepest dreams.

The ground laid in the first three steps prepares you for the real practice and action that you cultivate in Steps 4 to 9.

Step 4: Made a searching and fearless moral inventory of ourselves. Step 5: Admitted to God, to ourselves, and to another human being the exact nature of our wrongs. Steps 4 and 5 are practical expressions of Step 1, as well as of Tradition 1. They stress morals at a time when you are just freshly delivered from fear but still mindful of it in your guilt and in your sense of wrongdoing, both recent and remote. Early in the A.A. program you are still oriented to the traditional view of alcohol, which makes it a moral problem. You take Steps 4 and 5 with reference to the wrongs in the whole pattern of your behavior, not just your drinking. Concentration on the exact nature of your wrongs will mean search and study with the help of God as you understand Him and another human being.

Step 6: Were entirely ready to have God remove all these defects of character. Step 7: Humbly asked Him to remove our shortcomings. These steps represent a health exercise. You ask the intervention of God in the removal of defects. Observe the word "remove." The steps do not say destroy; they say remove. The removal of a defect can

mean that you place it in another context where it might
even prove useful. For example, your thirst can become
a thirst for a better way to live, a thirst for companionship,
a thirst for fun. Your sensitivity can become an awareness
of the value of freedom. Grandiose, you can become ideal-
istic about the prospect of more and more fellow alcoholics joining A.A.

In these steps you learn the art of being yourself, aware
of defects and shortcomings, ready to let the God of your
understanding remove these troubles, humbly asking
Him to do so. They are practical extensions of Step 2 and
Tradition 2.

*Step 8: Made a list of all persons we had harmed, and
became willing to make amends to them all. Step 9: Made
direct amends to such people wherever possible, except
when to do so would injure them or others.* These steps
are practical applications of the love you learn in Step 3.
They are taken in the effort to stay sober after you acquire
the desire to stop drinking—Tradition 3. They are demon-
strations of good will in action.

*Step 10: Continued to take personal inventory and
when we were wrong promptly admitted it.* Steps 9 and
10 remind you that you cannot drink again. Your personal
thirst, the longing to be your real self, cannot be
quenched with alcohol. This, down deep in your heart,
you know well from the memory of your misery. But
maybe once in a while you are tempted to put aside the
facts and try again to feel what it is to be drunk. That is
why St. Paul asks you to avoid the company of active
alcoholics as constant companions. But, you are to love
them, to help them, and to give them the A.A. message
if they want it.

Step 11: Sought through prayer and meditation to im-

prove our conscious contact with God as we understand Him, praying only for knowledge of His will for us and the power to carry that out. In Step 11 you continue to deepen your contact with God as you understand Him, constantly in search of His will and the power to carry it out. Once again it stresses your resourcefulness and inventive capacity.

Step 12: Having had a spiritual awakening as a result of these steps, we tried to carry this message to alcoholics, and to practice these principles in all our affairs. The spiritual awakening better enables you to carry the message of freedom, adventure, and love to other alcoholics and to practice the principles of all the steps in all affairs.

The "recap" steps (10, 11, 12) are more than restatements or summaries. "Recap" differs from repetition. It is a feeling of synthesis, of at-oneness. In this act there is recognition, better discipline of your problems, and deeper personal meaning. It is a dynamic return to earlier steps and traditions. The whole art is circular and active, not linear and static. The return in circular action is like the play of intention, technique, and practice in a creative personal design. In the personal design of sobriety the outcome in practice—feeling good—matches the intention in a kind of circular return to why you drank in the first place. Still, the return is always inventive and novel, not merely repetitious. If it were repetitious, you would drink again. But, in sobriety, the technique for feeling good is fellowship, a creative experience in which you go on learning until you die.

Recap is a use of memory for new creative insight and action. There is much that you repeat and stress again and again in any exercise of "recap." But always there emerges something novel and adventurous in the contact of dialogue and interaction of the last three steps.

To be free, resourceful, and friendly can never be a closed book. There is always another step to go. That is what you are reminded of in Steps 10, 11, and 12.

The Twelve Traditions

From start to finish the traditions stress the skill of anonymity, which is the main technique of A.A. fellowship.

Tradition 1: Our common welfare should come first; personal recovery depends upon A.A. unity. Step 1 leads to a sense of community, "our common welfare," to Tradition 1, which is the condition of your freedom.

Your freedom and your meaning emerge in group discussions and in personal activity based on insights revealed in the A.A. group. Intellectual improvement, better health, renewed interests, sharing with others of your problems, and helping others when aid is sought—all these essentials of good living merge in the kindly feeling of fellowship, brought together in free association by mutual consent. The personal meaning of each member and the freedom of those who slip and of those still to learn about A.A. depend on the harmony of group fellowship and the solid unity of the whole movement.

Tradition 2: For our group purposes there is but one ultimate authority—a loving God as He may express Himself in our group conscience. Our leaders are but trusted servants; they do not govern. Step 2, "came to believe," leads to the "loving God" of the second tradition. All the experience gathered in this tradition illustrates the skill of recognition. This skill involves your unity, one for all and all for one, your common feelings, your sense of community, your tears and laughter. In community you deepen at-oneness and insight into your common problem and purpose, your tragedy and joy. Step 2 and Tradition 2 are the condition of creative effort.

Each A.A. member carries a message bigger that all of us put together. You serve the message and its principles by acting as its vehicle. No one governs because all are servants. The only authority is the collective conscience of the group, the way the group as a whole reacts to new measures, suggestions, plans, and criticisms. If leaders emerge here and there, they will be men and women supported by the group, not by any personal dreams of power.

Tradition 3: The only requirement for A.A. membership is a desire to stop drinking. Step 3 and Tradition 3 make up the condition of love. "Made a decision" of Step 3 leads to "a desire to stop drinking" of the third tradition. Actually, the desire to stop drinking soon becomes the desire for fellowship. It is an early expression of a love that grows deeper as time goes by.

The only requirement for membership in A.A. is very simple. Any alcoholic who is aware of his problem and wants to do something about it is qualified to become an A.A. member.

Tradition 4: Each group should be autonomous except in matters affecting other groups or A.A. as a whole. Each group runs itself. It will respect the same autonomy in other groups, just as individual members respect the personal rights of fellow members in the same group. As a whole, A.A. is served by the Foundation, a cohesive organization that keeps groups in touch with one another and supplies literature and many sound suggestions.

Tradition 5: Each group has but one primary purpose —to carry its message to the alcoholic who still suffers. No other interest of any group should be greater than to carry the message of freedom to the alcoholic who still suffers. This thought should be kept uppermost when games, socials, business interests, personal ambitions, and resentments threaten a group's primary purpose.

Tradition 6: An A.A. group ought never endorse, finance or lend the A.A. name to any related facility or outside enterprise lest problems of money, property, and prestige divert us from our primary spiritual aim. As an A.A. member you know that money, property, and personal glory, either singly or together, can ruin the good of the A.A. movement—your sobriety and the prospective sobriety of those who still suffer from alcoholism. The advice is not to link publicly your materialistic activities as an ordinary citizen with the spiritual purpose of your life as an A.A. member.

Tradition 7: Every A.A. group ought to be fully self-supporting, declining outside contributions. This tradition is often dangerously ignored. You have to keep your identity as alcoholics, which you may lose if you accept the material support of those many well-meaning people who do not share your central problem. Alcoholics, during their long period of active drinking, are notoriously dependent on others. It is a part of the A.A. freedom plan that you stand on your own feet. Only one kind of contribution is sought from people outside of A.A.—it is their good will and the approval of what you are doing for yourself.

Tradition 8: Alcoholics Anonymous should remain forever nonprofessional, but our service centers may em-

ploy special workers. As A.A. members your efforts are amateur, in the best sense of that word. You do what you can out of love for the work because that work keeps you sober.

Professional and skilled people in various fields may be paid when such services would have to be paid for in any case. These paid workers are usually to be found in service centers. All regular A.A. efforts, centering around the carrying of the message to other alcoholics and helping members who have a "slip" problem, are freely and willingly given.

Tradition 9: A.A., as such, ought never be organized, but we may create service boards or committees directly responsible to those they serve. No one "joins" or "resigns" from A.A. It is a free and casual fellowship, with no organization. Any service boards and committees created have no power other than that vested in them by the groups, and they serve directly those to whom they are responsible.

Tradition 10: Alcoholics Anonymous has no opinion on outside issues; hence the A.A. name ought never be drawn into public controversy. A.A. has its hands full with its freedom program for alcoholics. Outside issues are not its concern. A.A. is not a religion; so there is no quarrel with the churches. It is not a political party; so there is no quarrel with government. It is not a science; so there is no quarrel with professors.

A.A. holds no controversial views about "wet" and "dry" philosophies. You only know that you, as alcoholics, cannot drink. Opinions about how much other people should or should not drink do not concern you as A.A. members.

Alcohol and God are the first things in your life as an A.A. member. It is alcohol as you knew it, and it is God as you understand Him. Alcohol takes second place when God comes first in A.A. About this there is no controversy. It is an act of faith.

To engage in public controversy is to betray an allegiance to values you prize more than your spiritual aim. If your spiritual aim is your primary interest, you will not be easily tempted to quarrel about secondary issues. There can be no quarrel about your primary aim—it is your faith and your life as an A.A. member.

Tradition 11: Our public relations policy is based on attraction rather than promotion; we need always maintain personal anonymity at the level of press, radio, and films. Advertisement is the essence of competitive living. It is all right in its place, but it is harmful in A.A. You cooperate in A.A.; you do not compete. You learn that to give is to receive what you need most, the trust and respect of your fellow members. You do not permit your name to be used in any mass media communication because personal glory may tempt you to forget your primary purpose.

Tradition 12: Anonymity is the spiritual foundation of all our traditions, ever reminding us to place principles above personalities. Anonymity basically means that you have no meaning by yourself, by right of your money, prestige, or self-exploits. You are a person, with meaning and identity, only by virtue of what takes you out of yourself to others. The second part of this tradition reminds you to place principles above personalities. This again stresses anonymity, because a personality, ever ego-conscious, proudly proclaims, "Here I am; look at me." Anything you stress as yours and yours alone is very unanonymous and becomes a sign for many people to respond to with fear, envy, or resentment. That is why "personalities" are often lonely, alienated from others, and, most of all, unfree. You find your real meaning by becoming a free, creative, and friendly person, not a personality.

Anonymity of service is more important than anonymity of the labels you use for personal names. The principles of honesty, humility, and compassion that you follow in your quiet unsung services are bigger than all A.A. members, either singly or taken together. Placing these principles above personality is the real meaning of anonymity. As long as you understand it in this way you need not fear your worst enemy, resentment, which can only arise when personalities clash.

Anonymity of names is secondary to anonymity of service, but important as long as there are people who are disdainful and morally critical of the alcoholic. Therefore, every member has the privilege to expect that his fellow members will not make it known that he is a member of A.A. As members grow in A.A. they usually come to see the true meaning of anonymity and lose the embarrassment associated with being a member of a fellowship that saved their lives.

The Personal Mystery

No one can tell another person how to be himself in the details of personal know-how. Such an effort would be a denial of the whole joy of personal unity. However, you can wondrously help one another in the art of personal meaning by sharing the *conditions* of personal identity.

The mystery of personal identity is that I am nothing by

myself. I can be a person only in contact with you. "I" really equals you and me. I do not give up my personal identity by needing you. I become truly myself in contact with you.

To accept this mystery is to shift from a logic of controls, the method of science, to personal know-how. This is a shift from distance to contact. The logic of science is objective; distance is required between knower and known. Contact is personal; it is knowledge in the action of touch, at-oneness.

The mystery of Alcoholics Anonymous strikes me in at least four main forms.

First is the A.A. "noncure" method as opposed to the cure approach of medical science. When you are sick from an organic disorder, such as cancer or heart trouble, you seek a cure. You go to a medical expert who prescribes a kind of treatment that you are expected to follow. This treatment then constitutes a control of the trouble. If you are lucky, the control will cure you. If you are less lucky, the control may keep the disorder from growing worse. However, every cure or control is accompanied by chronic fear—fear that the control will not work.

By contrast, in A.A. there is no cure, although the alcoholic may indeed become free in alcoholism. The great value of the fact that there is no cure is that there is no fear. If you accept the disorder completely, you need never fear any distress from the disorder because the complete acceptance of it will mean that you will never try to control it. The great personal value in this acceptance is that you will not be afraid.

The second kind of mystery is that you go to A.A. expecting to solve your problem. You have heard about the value of fellowship in coping with alcoholism. However, you discover in A.A. meetings that no great problems are ever solved; they are accepted. The acceptance of the problem, however, does not mean that you must continue to suffer from it. On the contrary, complete acceptance enables you to cope with the problem in a comfortable and satisfactory way. In the mystery of this acceptance, you learn to recognize your trouble and learn to be happy in the program that enables you to cope with it.

The manner in which you learn to accept your problem is found in this technique: you find yourself in others. You learn to recognize how you feel and how to discipline your feelings by recognizing those feelings in fellow alcoholics.

The third form of mystery in A.A. is that you learn to be sober for the same good reason that you first drank. You try to find in A.A. exactly what you tried to find in the bottle—to be happy, informal, relaxed, anonymous. The essence of this personal mystery is that you find your personal meaning in anonymity. You become free, adventurous, companionable; you relax; you learn to be yourself in the fellowship of A.A., which is grounded in anonymity.

A fourth form of mystery can be experienced in the twelfth tradition, where you are invited to put principles above personalities. Three negative principles are self-pity, resentment, and loneliness; and three positive ideals you reach toward are to be free, to be creative, to be loving. You put these six principles above personality in order to understand them, to discipline the first three, and to put into practice the last three.

The mystery about these principles is that although you are advised to put all of them above any personality considerations, the truth is that you observe these principles emerging in particular persons, including yourself. The principles are ahead of personalities and yet they are observed to emerge in persons. The principles are greater than the persons and therefore, in a sense, are impersonal. However, the principles depend upon persons for their expression.

The exciting discovery in A.A. is not so much the discovery of new ideas as the discovery of a technique. It is the way you do things in A.A. that makes it so exciting and valuable. The anonymous technique of A.A. goes beyond the self with all its fears.

Slogans

The slogans of Alcoholics Anonymous are excellent practical guidelines to enjoyment of the personal mystery.

First things first. The first thing in your life is sobriety. Everything else falls in second place. To be sober is to be free. To be free, you have to be in touch with your fellow alcoholic; no one can be free alone. To be in touch in fellowship is a spiritual experience based on common defects. These common defects are the drink habit and the tendencies to be dependent, resentful, and self-pitying. When you are in touch, you and many others, you learn to recognize your defects when you tell your personal stories to one another. After you learn what your defects are, and what you can do about them, you can never again take a drink unintentionally.

Easy does it. In the world today we all rush blindly toward any promise of instant comfort, instant pleasure, instant solutions to problems. However, A.A. says, "Take it easy. The best things come about by a wise, steady pursuit of freedom, a day at a time, over many years."

One thing is certain. You can stop drinking now, today, and begin anew the wonderful adventure of freedom that you can practice the rest of your life. You may be a new member of A.A., one of long standing, or one just thinking about joining. In any case, you know that alcoholics can stop drinking just as soon as they decide to do so. That much is definite, but remember that quality sobriety takes time.

Each new day, new month, new year in A.A. brings a wealth of free experience, joyous and spirited. You treasure your sobriety more and more as you learn from your fellow members and feel at depth the spiritual value of freedom. Yes, freedom is a spiritual experience because you have to get out of your own skin and reach toward others if you hope to be free. This takes you beyond yourself in the mystery of fellowship. Where there is fellowship, there is God, God as you understand Him.

The practice of "Easy does it" means not trying to control what you do, but rather to enjoy it. Control means fear, fear lest you fail to control. But "Easy does it" will always mean joy once you realize that whatever is good is never something that you want to finish or suppress. In pursuit of what is really good, you cannot expect too much too fast. Instead, it is better to relax and hope. Hope is prayer, not expectation.

Let go, and let God. When you turn your will and life over to God as you understand Him, you become free because you become responsible. "Letting" God does not mean you cease creative effort. On the contrary, letting go and letting God means to exert all the talent you have, and then some.

Letting God into your life means receiving the gift of freedom. You become free to do many creative things that you were unable to do when you drank. You go beyond the controls that alcohol inflicted upon your behavior and beyond the controls that you tried to impose on yourself and others. Beyond these controls is the freedom you find in fellowship. This fellowship of A.A. is what you create when you "Let go, and let God." When you say "Hope, don't expect," you do not mean "Stop all action and let God do it." Letting God do it means expressing the best that is in you, and that is action.

A day at a time. You cannot become completely sober in all the deep riches of sobriety in one day. You cannot dry up your fellow alcoholic in a twelve-step effort all at once. "Sufficient unto the day is the evil thereof." There are enough problems in one day to cope with. It is a waste of good energy to try to solve the problems of a lifetime in a day, a week, a year.

You are sober one day at a time. Tomorrow is not here, yesterday is gone forever. Today is always. Today is the eternal "now." Live it freely and happily and hope that tomorrow will be as good as today. Hope, not expect, it to be just as you desire. Hope is a religious feeling, but expectation, when thwarted, brings bitterness. Hope is faith, and faith is life.

"A day at a time" is easiest to understand when you discover that living is an art; so too is sobriety. No art is ever finished. Always there is more to practice, more to discipline, more to create. Because sobriety is an art and a lifetime experience, you savor it best a day at a time and in the relaxed loosening of controls in "Easy does it."

Think. Every thought is a feeling understood. Every

feeling expressed is an action. Thinking is the art of becoming aware of the way you feel.

To think creatively is to think in action outside the boundaries of your own skin. To think reflectively is only good when you recognize a problem to be a chance to do something exciting, new, adventurous. When thinking is neither a knowing in action nor a recognition of something in a new light, it is fantasy with no foothold in real life.

At best, to think is to love. The more confused your thinking, the fuzzier is its object. The clearer your thinking the more certain you are of what you are devoted to. What you love is what you concentrate on. Your sobriety, for example, is an act of love if you stay sober. It is an act of indifference if you slip and continue to slip. If you fight to stay sober, you'll probably drink because fighting is not loving. Fighting alcohol is fearful. If you are afraid to drink, almost certainly you will do so until you learn to respect alcohol, accept it as alcoholism for you, and until you learn to love sobriety as much as you once loved to drink.

There is no need to think about alcohol except as a road to sobriety. You don't have to fight or fear it. Your thoughts about alcohol are creative if they lead you always to the fact that you are alcoholic. This fact, thought about again and again, is the gateway to your freedom and opens up your capacity to love.

Live and let live. Every resentment, every criticism, is an attack on your fellow man. It is also an attack on yourself. So you cripple your own life and destroy yourself by inches each time you feel resentment, distrust, or hatred.

The only way you can be free is to be as sure as you can

that your fellow members are also free. Your limits are the limits of your associates. You do nothing to remove your limits if you do nothing to help others remove theirs. To do this is to live and let live and keep an open mind.

The slogan can also be expressed the other way around: Let live and live. You live best and most freely only if you let the other fellow do the same. How do you let him live? By accepting him just as you find him, without fear and without criticism.

But for the grace of God. The grace of God is the loss of desire to drink, and that is the same as the loss of fear. To drink is to be afraid, afraid because you do not like yourself the way you are. Not liking yourself is the same as being afraid of yourself.

But if you no longer fear yourself, if you can accept yourself just as you are, you do not need to drink. You lose the desire to drink when the need is gone. You get a second chance at the joy of life in the grace of God, which now means the capacity to change.

The grace of God turns the losses of support, control, and self-sufficiency into great values. Loss of support enables you to be free in your friendship with others. Loss of control inspires you to do for yourself what you once could not do; you become creative. Loss of self-sufficiency convinces you that the only way you can live your life fully and richly is in fellowship with your fellow alcoholics.

Keep it simple. Saying and doing things the hard way is often a sign of uncertainty, of doubt, of dodging the facts. When you are sure of something, you find a simple way to understand, accept, and express it. "I am an alcoholic. I can't drink." This is a much simpler explanation of your problem than a profound definition of alcoholism or a complex of words explaining why you cannot drink. "I can be sober, free, happy in the practice of A.A. principles." This is much simpler than the study of the defects of "personality" in psychotherapy courses designed to make you "mature."

One drink is too many, a thousand not enough. Nothing could be simpler, more incisive than this truth for alcoholics. It supports the first step of A.A. and makes it clear that the alcoholic who still wants to drink with control is deceiving himself at depth. Actually, the desire to drink with control only shows how alcoholic a person is— a drinker who would like to drink a thousand more but is afraid to do so. The fearful need to use control shows that one drink is already too many.

Utilize, don't analyze. This slogan does not discredit thinking, but it does stress creative thinking. Be inventive and resourceful, be practical. Don't engage in logic chopping. Use and produce!

What counts is what you learn after you know it all. Many of us easily grow smug after years in the A.A. program. This slogan takes you back to Step 2 over and over again. What do you believe today? Is it the same as yesterday? The slogan also takes you to Steps 10, 11, and 12 as new adventures every day. And when you are sure you have a pretty good grip on the whole program, you relax and remember that what counts still lies ahead.

Turn it over. This is a constant reminder of Step 3, in my view the most dynamic step of the whole A.A. program. Every day you must be sure that your will and your life have been given over to the care of God as you understand Him, not as someone says you should understand

Him, but as you deeply feel Him as genuine and active in your life.

Prayers

Prayer is an expression of acceptance, hope, and fulfillment of being. Through it you achieve integrity with yourself, with others, and with God as you know Him. In this sense, as an A.A. member, you pray as you express yourself in actions of good will among your associates. Your actions in sobriety reveal the capacity to accept, to hope, and to find at-oneness. In thought, action, and prayer you show gratitude, and more than anything else you are grateful.

As an A.A. member you find that prayer is downright practical. Through it you become better acquainted with God and with yourself.

Prayer illustrates the art of empathy, a search for the ideal feeling of at-oneness that every human being thirsts for. That search for integrity as an A.A. member is well expressed in this verse that hangs on the wall of the hospital chapel at Brighton, Michigan: "I sought my soul, my soul I could not see. I sought my God and he eluded me. I sought my brother and I found all three."

Over the years four prayers have grown in common use among A.A. members—the serenity prayer, the 23rd psalm, the prayer of St. Francis, and the Lord's Prayer.

Serenity Prayer. The serenity prayer, which is universal in its appeal, is a request for serenity, courage, and wisdom. It is a simple prayer, containing tremendous wisdom —everything really "begins with me."

God grant me the serenity to accept the things I cannot change, courage to change the things I can, and the wisdom to know the difference.

The 23rd Psalm. This is an expression of faith that you are never alone. It expresses the themes of joy, acceptance, and endurance through every kind of hardship in the faith that you are one with God. You might have to do without much that you desire, but your faith enables you to accept whatever may happen to you.

The Lord is my shepherd, I shall not want. He maketh me to lie down in green pastures, He leadeth me beside the still waters. He restoreth my soul. He leadeth me in the paths of righteousness for His name sake. Yea, though I walk through the valley of the shadow of death, I will fear no evil for thou art with me. Thy rod and thy staff, they comfort me. Thou preparest a table before me in the presence of mine enemies. Thou anointest my head with oil, my cup runneth over. Surely goodness and mercy shall follow me all the days of my life and I will dwell in the house of the Lord forever.

The Prayer of St. Francis. This prayer is a masterpiece of love all the way. In it you do not ask God for things, you ask for states of being in which you can be active and productive and creative. Through it you search for the reality of being rather than for the defects of having.

Lord, make me an instrument of Thy peace.
Where there is hatred let me sow love;
where there is wrong, let me bring forgiveness;
where there is discord, let me bring harmony;

where there is error, truth;
where there is doubt, faith;
where there is despair, hope;
where there is darkness, light;
where there is sadness, joy.
Grant that I may not so much seek to be consoled
as to console, to be loved as to love, for it is
in giving that we receive, it is in pardoning
that we are pardoned, it is in dying that we are
born to eternal life.

St. Francis clearly saw that all our troubles are love disorders. The corrective is not to attack but to harmonize. It is better to console, to understand, to love than to be a recipient of those blessings. Those blessings come if you first make sure that you can give them.

The Lord's Prayer. This prayer is a request for sustenance, for forgiveness in the measure that we forgive, for a way out of temptation, and for deliverance from evil. It is marked by "our," "we," "us," and "Thy will." The stress is on personal identity as felt in fellowship with others.

Our father, who art in heaven Hallowed be Thy name. Thy kingdom come, Thy will be done on earth as it is in heaven. Give us this day our daily bread. Forgive us our debts as we forgive our debtors. Lead us not into temptation, but deliver us from evil.

Simone Weil, in *Waiting on God,* expresses the belief that the Lord's Prayer contains all possible petitions. "We cannot conceive," she says, "of any prayer which is not already contained in it. It is to prayer what Christ is to humanity. It is impossible to say it once through giving the fullest possible attention to each word, without a change, infinitesimal, perhaps, but real, taking place in the soul."

Chapter 6

Personal Know-How

Defense, Control, and Personal Art

To break down defenses, to confront you with *your* problem, is to modify your habit. Whether imposed by yourself or by an external authority, behavior modification is a form of control. The basic idea is that you, the "patient," have been sick and must become "well." In this context, "well" is an ideal of behavior prescribed by a therapist or a moralist whose statistics must show that the controls have worked. Such a treatment does not respect the personal mystery of freedom, of art, of love. Rather, it is an effort to reduce the personal mystery and make the treatment plan work. How? By accurate planning, by controls, and by evidence of statistics.

A sobriety program based on self-control (the higher must-nots defeat the lower desires) or on external control (such as in contract, confrontation, and "hot seat" techniques) is based on determining what is good for you in an accurate, objective plan of treatment. The result is either a grim, rigid moral system or a "statistically sound" treatment. In both there is the dogma of what is objectively good. Both are founded on the control principle, which always implies the controller and the controlled.

Any treatment approach based on the control principle can only result in a totalitarian type "cure." "Patients" will get "better" by suffering a greater loss of freedom than they experienced in the disorder.

If addiction is a control problem, then a control technique can do nothing but worsen the addiction. As an alcoholic, you are already overcontrolled. You are an individual in chronic conflict, with the one side of you trying to control, or dominate, the other side. Control perpetuates your basic problem.

Rather than moral systems and scientific treatments that keep you divided, we need something that integrates you if that is what you want. How are you to become integrated, at one with yourself and at one with others? Through personal art and the personal know-how that puts that art into practice.

Personal know-how is not a treatment, not a cure, not a psychological tool. It is not a science, not a morality. It is not objective; it is personal. It is the art of knowing yourself through your fellow man. As in every art, the action comes first; the thinking follows the action or occurs within it.

Personal know-how illustrates its unifying quality in the first stage of the art, contact. As an alcoholic in distress you will want to feel some reason to make contact. After all, a reason is the image of an end in view, and you naturally want to know what personal know-how will require of you and where it will take you. In making contact you do something about your drinking and about finding that reason you seek.

An intention will arise from your contact with other alcoholics and through your memory of your own drinking behavior. The intention will be the desire to stop drinking, combined with the purpose of becoming sober. The basic reason for drinking will become unified with the basic reason for sobriety, the longing to feel good.

What brings you to the decision to be sober for the same reason you used to drink? The evidence of thousands like you assures you there is nothing wrong with what you were, nothing wrong with the reason for drinking when it was joyous. You are assured by fellow A.A. members that you may still intend a program of living based on the reason for drinking before trouble set in.

In hanging on to that reason you feel the conflict between what you originally sought and what you now get from drinking. And you realize well that you must try another way simply because the drinking routine failed you.

A reason is an explanation of past, present, or proposed action—an explanation, which is sound, contrasted with an alibi, which is unsound. An intention is a plan of action, pointing to the technique that will implement the intention and the practice that will complete the meaning.

An intention embraces a desire and a purpose, sometimes in the service of reason, sometimes not. When the intention serves the reason, you behave deliberately in a disciplined way. Your purpose will guide your desire, all in harmony with the reason. So it can be in a sobriety program. Wanting to feel good is the reason. Being sober is the purpose and stopping drinking, as well as staying stopped, is the desire.

When the intention does not serve any reason, you may well behave creatively in a spirit of exploration. Your actions may be taken just for the fun of it. Then you behave wholeheartedly and you are integrated, unimpeded by fear or doubt or controls. After you are well skilled in the techniques of personal know-how, the adventure of sobriety will come to mean living for the joy of it.

There is no good reason why everything must have a reason, beforehand. All adventurous action is done spontaneously, with intention and some prospect of joy or truth but without any definite plan. You only stop to think and find reasons when you have distressing problems. Then, of course, you reflect on your behavior to locate and clarify your reasons and your intentions.

Behavior you can change is behavior for which you find a reason. If you could not find a reason for drinking in the "good old days," your drinking was not an action but an event. A sickness, for example, is an event contrasted with art, an action. An event happens. An action is done with desire, on purpose.

As an alcoholic you begin drinking as an agent, a person able to make choices. You act intentionally. As an agent, you are an artist, fashioning a way of life that you first find beautiful. You are not concerned with either moral goodness or prudent health measures. Although drinking begins as an art, it becomes a sickness when the event of addiction befalls. *The sickness is an accident on the way to meaning.*

In practice, alcoholism is an addiction that functions between event and action, more driven by event than by action. It is an art that went wrong, got lost in the event of sickness and in those lapses of action where creative effort degenerated into moral offenses. Within the event of alcoholism, however, there is evidence of some choice-making, some action. As an active alcoholic you can go to

a bar and order drinks. You can choose to drink \
home, or elsewhere; whatever you do, you want \

The aim of personal know-how is to restore you.
ing to live beautifully, to feel good in the practice of personal art rather than in the practice of alcoholism. Personal art lies between event and action, but it is more
inspired by action than driven by event. It is concerned
with discovery of meaning in life through relationships
with fellow alcoholics in the common concern of alcoholism. It is creative and resourceful, less concerned with
moral must-nots than with the prospect of exciting new
experiences.

To be alcoholic and to be sober at the same time is not
the conflict that many suppose it to be and try to treat. It
is a state of harmony between two different life styles
whose main reason is the same—the longing to feel good.
This longing unites me with you in what it means to be
a person. I cannot be a person by myself. I need you and
other persons and things as nearly like they really are as
possible. If I am to be I, then you have to be you, and all
others—my disorder, other people and things—have also
to be themselves. My being includes the being of you and
everyone and everything else. Why? Because I am me,
you, my problem, and "it." The anonymous "it" includes
everything in the world within reach not to be had, measured, or controlled but to *be* as it is in itself—something
I can feel as nearly like itself as possible.

Where Personal Know-How Begins
Personal know-how begins with what I want. As men-
tioned, "I" includes myself, you, and my problem. My
problem, alcoholism, is not something I have. Being alco-

holic is something I am. Similarly, my relation to you is not something I have. What I do to you, for you, with you is something I am.

What I want is to do something about my habit, my addiction. What I want is to restore purpose to my habit. In active addiction my original purpose, to feel good, dwindled away. Therefore, addiction is a habit with a lost purpose. To restore the purpose of feeling good to my habit is not to break or control it but to extend, deepen, enrich it, and make it meaningful again.

The new purpose will be to become sober, supported by the desire to stop drinking. Together, the purpose and desire provide me with an intention. This intention will concern the art of being myself, of being sober, in order to feel good.

I simply intend to fulfill this original intention by switching from having to being. The habit of wanting to feel good continues. Nothing is broken in the habit, nothing modified by containing, controlling, or moderating the habit. On the contrary, something is added: that is the purpose that got lost in active alcoholism.

First of all, to feel good I must be free. That brings you into the picture of personal know-how. I cannot be free and I cannot be a person without you. You replace my old desire to drink. To switch from having to being means that I cannot have or control you any more than I could have or control alcohol.

My problem was not merely the mistake of having alcohol. It was, and is, the entire problem of having. That includes control treatments, experts, authorities, as well as pills and alcohol. It includes everything I strive to have and be "had" by. I propose to limit the extent of my being "had" to my addiction.

The desire to know you, to know others, now replaces the desire to drink. I propose to be sober to replace the original purpose of feeling good. I now invest the purpose of feeling good with a deliberate aim toward sobriety. In a program of sobriety I deepen the longing to feel good. I give it vastly better discipline.

The guiding principles of personal know-how represent the being life style. Compare and contrast the intentions, techniques, and outcomes that make up these principles with those of dependence, control, ego, alcoholism, and prestige (see page 14). Since the intentions here match the outcomes, each principle has a sound meaning.

Observe in Table 4 that fellowship and anonymity are principles as well as techniques. The technique of fellowship is developed in anonymity, and the technique of anonymity is exercised in fellowship.

Table 4

GUIDING PRINCIPLES OF THE BEING LIFE STYLE

Principle	Intention	Technique	Outcome
Action (agent)	to be free	contact	free, accepting, interpersonal
Adventure (artist)	to be adventurous	recognition	creative, resourceful
Fellowship (friend)	to be a person	acquaintance in anonymity	loving, being yourself
Sobriety	to feel good	abstinence and personal know-how	feeling good, creative, free, loving
Anonymity	to be yourself	fellowship	adventurous, sobriety, self-realization

Contact

The intention of being sober involves a technique, contact. To contact you is to reveal interest in your present feelings, actions, and possible feelings to come. Contact is a distinctly free act, free from absorption with my own needs, free to savor your feelings, needs, actions. This does not mean to inhibit or deny my own needs and feelings. It means temporary detachment from them in order to feel them in you. In the dynamics of contact, I am detached from these driving urges only the better to get in touch with them for renewed creative effort.

In contact, touch and detachment alternate. The action in contact highlights the value of resistance. "Resistance" is used here in its original meaning, contact by touch. Without the resistance I feel in touch with you, or anything else, I could not in detachment reflect on the meaning of that touch.

The genuine feeling that tells me that I am I and you are you when we are in real touch is resistance. Resistance is not defensive, not opposing. To resist is to be in touch, not in combat. Fighting and control efforts may arise from resistance, but these stem from fearing the resistance. If resistance is accepted and respected, it can be the initial phase of creative action.

The "it" that became alcoholism would never have occurred in my life if I had not already failed to attain harmony with you, my fellow man. When I first drank I was amiable with you, the "you" without whom I could not feel good. That changed dramatically. Centered more and more on my isolated self, I lost my enjoyment of you. Also I began to see you as a threat to me, for a thousand different reasons, all of them fearful. I not only lost you when you became a threat, I also forgot I really needed you in order to be a real person. In the distress of active alcoholism, I became a self, an ego-bound creature, out of touch with you, out of contact with the "other than I." That is why alcoholism is a love disorder. Love is always for the other. Self-love, without positive regard for others, is self-intoxication. It is self-alienation.

There is a direct relationship between my alienation from you and the deepening of my alcoholism. Having alcohol and being had by "it" more and more replaced you in my life. My fear of you went hand in hand with my fear of drinking. As one grew, so did the other.

In the experience of resistance, with its rhythm of touch and detachment, I come to know "it" and you too. I accept my alcoholism as I accept you. In touch I am in action with you, and I learn to be free. Detached from you I reflect on what our touch was, on the alcoholism we share, on my personal meaning, and on what lies ahead in the adventure of living.

To try to destroy your place in my personal life is as false as trying to break my habit. Why? Because I *am* you *and* my habit. "I" always means being in contact with you, in an ongoing relationship between you and me. Even in the detachment phase of contact I am aware of thinking about you and of my return to resume touch with you.

It is tough to cope with the problem feature of my addiction if I want to make changes for a reason different from the reason I first drank. To break or modify my habit is an attempt to inhibit the desire to drink, the desire to feel good.

The three forms of inhibition—support, control, and surrender—never work because they directly destroy or weaken my relationship with you.

In seeking support, I turn to you time and again. I seek

ways out of my problem by my excuses, alibis, and use of
the blame-placing ploy: it's my wife, it's you, it's my boss
who fail to understand me; it's my health. Such are my
supports. I do not give you the respect you deserve if I
expect you to believe me and give your support to these
defensive signs.

In surrender I become committed to drinking if I com-
mit myself to you. If I surrender to you in your demand
that I be abstinent, it is only a matter of time until I am
drinking again. I can be sober only if I wholeheartedly
want to be. Sobriety is an act of love, not one of submission
or surrender. To surrender to you, or you to me, is a
weakening of our personal relationship, where ideally we
live in harmony, not in conflict or submission.

When I try to control your drinking behavior, or you try
to control mine, I run into trouble. Control efforts are
always accompanied by fear, which cripples freedom and
leads to addictive type behavior.

I may even try to impose control on myself—submitting
in part to drinking, in part to abstinence. This brings
about a state of chronic conflict within myself, and in that
distressed state I can have no satisfactory relationship
with you.

Control combines the gloom of denial and the shortsightedness of surrender. The gloom of denial is to suppose that drinking is all bad; therefore I won't admit there
is a problem. The shortsightedness of surrender is to think
only of the value of drinking but not of all its misery.
Control is miserable because, ridden with fear, there is no
prospect of any joy except the grim hope of conquest.

Fear accounts for support, surrender, and control. In
the habit-modifying approach, the denial technique, fear

is felt because of the prospect of pain. In surrender, fear is felt in the interest of pleasure. In control, the alcoholic is afraid of both pain and pleasure.

Joyful sobriety cannot be based on either the avoidance of pain, the plan for pleasure, or the control of both pain and pleasure. Both avoidance of pain and pursuit of pleasure are features of the "having" philosophy. If I know the whole truth of the drinking problem, I will be aware of both its joy and its misery and of the integrity I seek beyond them.

I accept the desire to drink just as I accept my habit of wanting to feel good. My problem is not that of opposing the desire to drink to the desire to stop drinking. Rather, my problem is the adventure of harmonizing the two desires.

They are felt to be in harmony when I realize that both desires arise from the habit of wanting to feel good. This is important! I do not become aware of the desire to feel good until after the desire to drink and my drinking practice prove that I finally felt worse in most ways, most of the time, from drinking.

My reflection on this experience, in the detachment phase of contact, initiates a choice. The choice, the capacity to do one thing rather than another, comes from my contact with you and from my reflection on it. The improvement of my thinking enables me to see that when I used to drink I was not at that time aware of any clear reason—I drank just for the fun of it. Now a reason emerges—drinking comes to mean drinking in order to feel good.

Aristotle said that a choice is a "reason that desires or a desire that reasons." Now that I have a reason for my

early drinking I may desire something other than the
routine that failed me. I may say, "In order to feel good,
I desire to stop drinking."

I could, of course, drink again. But I don't have to do so
because what I am addicted to is the reason for drinking,
not drinking itself.

As an alcoholic I can now say, "The reason for not drinking is to feel good." Therefore, I desire to stop drinking.
The desire to stop drinking is matched by the purpose of
being and staying sober—all in order to feel good. I need
not worry about the loss of desire to drink. All kinds of
other desires will compete for my attention, keeping me
busier and more amused than I ever was.

Through contact with you, I discover that to feel good
I have to be myself, as a person. That means to be in a
positive relationship with you and my problem.

Recognition

The recognition of my feelings and fears in you releases
me from being governed by them in my own behavior.
What makes insight possible is the experience of contact.
After getting in touch with you on the basis of our common interest, freedom, I become detached from my own
misery and fear when I recognize my problem in you.
This recognition does not remove the problem, but it
wondrously reduces the misery and fear. The problem
remains as our common ground of communication and of
the source of our creative effort. We cultivate personal
artistry in the central feature of personal know-how, the
skill of recognition.

The awareness of our unity with other persons and the
play of fellow feeling among us are the first two forms of
recognition in personal know-how.

If we are in conflict with ourselves, we will be in conflict with others and confused about our drinking problem. Divided within and trying to control ourselves, we will find others equally divided and will try to control them too.

An unresolved conflict within ourselves breeds an illusion harmful to friends and enemies alike. The illusion will make the friends appear closer than they really are and the enemies more fearful than they really are. A conflict also accounts for our fear of alcohol and our attack upon it either by a moral or scientific attitude toward it. The threat we feel from other people or from alcohol is a reflection of the divided self.

The first thing to do when we feel such a conflict is to recall that our drinking behavior and our sober aim are more in harmony than we suspected.

To savor a better integrated sense of being we need to recall our childhood and youth—the feelings we knew before the rivalries of school, of competition, of work, and of love. This is not psychoanalytic, not an effort to explain the present in terms of the past. It is simply to recognize an ageless longing. Whether six or sixty, you and I want to be at one personally, each with himself and with others. In this act of recognition we harmonize what we wanted then with what we want now.

Drinking was an effort to "get it together" in stressful periods of conflict, fear, or divided love, or just for the fun of it. Then the practice deteriorated into conflict deeper than ever.

Becoming aware of basic unity is an exercise in integration. We recognize the essential unity of what we wanted when we drank and what we want now. *This act of integration is essential to our becoming free.* A divided self cannot be free. This we feel in the relaxing truth that you and I stop drinking for the same good reasons that we drank in the first place. Our sharing of this truth gives us a doubly confirmed unity. We are at one with each other in sharing a past and a present. Our intentions are in a basic unity. "What it used to be like" is excitingly similar to "What it is like now." Both the past and the present reveal that we both want the same thing for ourselves. Everything we want depends on our unity, you with me, both of us with others, in quest of our common freedom.

Our drinking routine turned out to be disastrous. But that was not our intention. We did not have much of an intention at all when we began drinking. It is only when we look back and compare notes in fellow feeling that we make a fair guess that we drank to feel good, or at least a little less miserable. We recognize that an activity endowed with a clear, wise intention will fare better than a haphazard routine that ends in misery.

That brings us to a sense of community, where intentions flourish best. A shared intention, tested by many, will stand up dramatically better than an intention or desire kept to yourself.

A community, a group with common interests, exists within society. The rule of society is law. The principle of a community is personal know-how. As members of a community, we are obliged to accept the ways of the society we belong to. Society deals with matters of fact such as we see in law, applied science, and all organized measures designed for our comfort, satisfaction, and safety. Such measures concern the handling of money, the earning of power, the exercise of sex. As members of a community we are also concerned with matters of intention. Intentions refer to our ideals such as the longing to be free, to enjoy adventure and art, to know love.

Society exists for our protection, to cope with the threats, potential in each of us, that we pose to one another. Society controls us because of our fear of one another. The controls must be reliable and strong. In the name of society we pursue science and apply it where we can, we frame norms of behavior, we provide food and shelter according to the rules of commerce. Society is run on a common restraint, in accordance with law and custom.

A community exists for the sake of friendship to discipline the need I have for you. It is not organized. It is based, not on science, not on objective methods of knowledge, but on personal know-how. The basic unit of personal know-how is two persons in community, in relation to a common other that includes them. For you and me the "common other" is our alcoholism and its potential capacity to become sobriety. Also the "common other" includes the mysterious world of all that is anonymous.

Personal art flourishes in community because only in community can we be truly free, creative, and loving. Tragedy and humor are experiences essential to a rich sense of community. They are to be valued, most of all, for themselves, but they are also feelings of practical value.

The uninvited tragedy of our drinking in its sick stage we communicate to one another in our stories, in community feeling. This is the tragic sequel that teaches us, without question, that we cannot drink again. This value is positive in opening the way to new-found freedom. Being free is first based on what we cannot do.

Humor and tragedy furnish us with the limits that guide

our sober freedom. Every freedom program has its discipline. In it we are entertained as well as instructed.

The Tragedy of Alcohol. We learn to recognize these facts about alcohol, ourselves, and tragedy: (1) alcohol brings the opposite of its early promise; (2) if you are an alcoholic, you always will be one; alcoholism is a tragic fact; (3) active alcoholism can kill if you stay with it; (4) as an alcoholic you are susceptible to addiction in other areas such as drugs and the routines of the leaner, schemer, and loner; (5) the main value of tragedy is that it can be a gateway to your freedom in many areas; the admission of loss of control leads to creative effort.

The Humor of Sobriety. We also learn these facts about the humor of sobriety: (1) sobriety is not the opposite of thirst; it is its fulfillment; (2) you do not break your habit; you add to it; you are sober for the same good reason you drank—to feel good; but now you give your habit the benefit of a purpose that makes you feel even better; that purpose is to feel good without feeling bad; (3) addiction is the logical outcome of the unanonymous way of life with its overcontrol; (4) alcoholism eventually leads to sobriety; the only way to get what you want out of drinking is to become sober; (5) sobriety is not an adjustment to everyday life; it is an adventure going beyond the daily routine, in which you become free, resourceful, amiable.

In the skills of recognition we learn that our lives are not a possession nor are they something we are all by ourselves. Each of us exists in a polarity of "I and you" united by a common "other," our alcoholism in our sobriety, grounded in the exciting open area of all that is anonymous. That is the personal mystery. We exist by trust in each other and in the anonymous world that underlies

and surrounds our faith in love. What we are, as contrasted with what we have, is a gift. We have to believe
that the gift is worthwhile, even though most of what we
do and most of what we mean is founded on anonymity.

Fellowship

In fellowship we cultivate intimacy and respect. Here
we find acquaintance, the essence of personal know-how,
which is the art of living with others anonymously in creative trust, in growing acquaintance.

The condition basic to this miracle is that the group be
a fellowship of fellow sufferers, fellow students. No one is
a master, expert, or leader, for such a posture inhibits
personal art. I cannot see my problem in you if you appear
as an expert who knows better, who has his problem "mas-
tered."

The informal nature of fellowship fosters a nonau-
thoritarian, personal attitude toward all problems. The
informal, spontaneous feeling in fellowship is also known
by the term "anonymous."

A.A. fellowship is free of fear stemming from defensive
desires because it is sparked and sustained in the good
disposition. In an offhand way, when my guard is down,
I see something in you that I recognize. Good will
flourishes in this recognition. A sustained effort enables
me to discipline and extend the habit of good will, which
takes me out of myself, my fearful protected self, to the
adventure of knowing you. Good will is not separate and
distinct from human self-will. It is what I feel when I
recognize my desires and fears in you. That recognition,
and the empathy exercised, constitutes an act of good will.
This is how we learn to become friends.

To be anonymous is to be indifferent to what we have but deeply concerned with what we are. What we are is a constant becoming. That is why it is hard to name the anonymous. There are, however, practical clues. Striving to be free, constantly seeking new insight, searching for joy and adventure, learning better how to love—all these efforts are personal, all are interpersonal, all are anonymous.

Science, as we know it, cannot guide us in knowing one another as persons. Why? Because a person is a subject, an object, and "it" at the same time. As subject, I am I. As object, I am "you." Also I am my disorder, my problem, as I discipline "it" anonymously.

Science requires distance between subject and object: the one controls; the other, in perspective, is controlled, whether the other is "you" or the disorder. If I am controlled by you, I am not a person. A human being, a patient, a victim, maybe, but not a person.

I can only know you, as a person, by getting acquainted with you. That means, first, to get in touch with you, recognize myself in you, and put trust in the prospect of our friendship.

Friendship is about love, love beyond the angles of money, power, and sex. Now the desire to stop drinking, the purpose of becoming and staying sober, and the acceptance of the common problem of alcoholism are conditions of friendship between you and me. Why? Because sobriety has to be an act of love if it is to discipline our love disorder. Its remedy must be the kind of love we have always longed for but failed to find.

The extension of our friendship into a wider area to include others becomes a fellowship. Best of all, fellowship brings us freedom. Our personal freedom depends on our unity in fellowship.

Fellowship gives us adventure and joys we never thought possible in the self-centered days of our drinking. We used to think we had to look out primarily for ourselves. Now we learn that the adventure of life is found in the "other." You and my problem and all that I do not yet know make up "the other."

In fellowship I care for myself as I care for you, for the mystery of the problem that we share. Our alcoholism is bigger than we are; it afflicts millions like us. No one of us, by himself, can do anything about it. It is beyond anything we can manage or isolate for self-control.

We must constantly practice the principles of fellowship, respect and intimacy. Each of us must respect others as much as we become intimate and friendly with them. We could lose our freedom if our trust falters, if fear creeps into our activities. In our mutual respect, we constantly remember that it is better to accept than to judge. To judge is to criticize, to make the other fearful. To try to control is equally fear inducing, and fear cripples productive action and destroys our freedom.

Fellowship is an activity with stress on being. It exists for the purpose of each A.A. member to be himself in the fullness of his nature. Each member discovers that to be himself is to care for the other and to learn to love.

My fear of you and of my alcoholism is the fear of life itself. Another way of saying this is, "My biggest problem comes from my fear of people and my fear of nature." Both people and nature (my addiction follows natural law) have their source in something other that I either fear or learn to love.

In fellowship I come to respect and then to love the anonymous source of both people and nature. I also learn that if we trust each other we can create ways of living that put us in harmony with one another and nature as we find it. God, the greater power, the life force, "the other" are various names for our belief in something other than ourselves. All have in common the mysterious quality we call anonymous.

The desire to drink evaporates in the steady practice of fellowship, where we learn to be free daily and feel what joy and love we deserve. Freedom does not keep, no more than joy or love does, unless we renew it each day. I believe that is what our request for "daily bread" means in the Lord's Prayer. We never have more than enough to last us each day.

We all need to be in fellowship with others because we are all so human. We can easily revert to the practices of a leaner, schemer, and loner. We can easily fall into the routines of blame placing, controlling, and withdrawing. It helps enormously to know that we cannot fight our human nature. We must realize that we can be both leaner and free agent, con man and creator, loner and lover at the same time. Each of is a human being and a person at the same time, an ambivalent creature in transition to we know not what.

As long as we are in fellowship, the person in us will be our discipline. The discipline of our trouble lies not in any neat, ready-made plan outside ourselves. Each of us must feel "It begins with me."

To be free again, adventurous again, friendly again are the joys found in fellowship. We find these when we learn to carry the message to other alcoholics. In practicing personal know-how in everyday life we will approach all problems and adventures in the same way as we discipline our alcoholic disorder. We will learn to treat other people as we treat our fellow alcoholics—with acceptance, intimacy, and respect.

Chapter 7

The "Slip" Problem

"First Things First"

As alcoholics we are all capable of a "slip," a relapse into our drinking routine. When so inclined, it is wise to review the first five steps of the AA program.

Without question and with a whole heart, we must accept the truth of Step 1, "powerless over alcohol." There is no way we can justify even one drink. But there is more. Our lives are "unmanageable."

The great note of hope is in Step 2, when we turn from our proud, fearful selves to a Power greater than ourselves, the whole adventure of the mysterious unknown. Whenever we grow smug, we need to remember that "What counts is what we learn after we know it all." The capacity to laugh at our pretensions enables us to be humble enough to go on learning, to be trainable, "down to earth," open, ready for new adventure.

The practical worth of the good disposition is embodied in Step 3, where we decide to turn our will and our life over to God as we understand Him. We will have no urge to drink if we remember to practice the good will we learn from our A.A. group, and also combine that good will with acceptance and hope.

The self-study or moral inventory of ourselves in Step 4 and the compassion of Step 5, where we admit to God, ourselves, and another person the exact nature of our wrongs, take us further along the free and easy way of sobriety. These steps reach into our hidden fears and tensions, releasing them, bringing them into light, which is essential to eliminating them.

We are all subject to low feelings that challenge our faith. Sometimes all we have is the sharing of our bitterness. But even that helps. George Santayana offers us good advice, "Here is disillusionment. Take it and be happy." Disillusionment is where our happiness begins. The deceits of life are often the ground of our hope.

Some of us are drink slippers and some are think slippers. One leads to the other. A drink slipper wants to drink and does so. A think slipper wants to drink but does not—just now. Still, the wish is father of the thought, and the thought is father of the deed.

Think slippers are of two kinds. The first wants to drink but refrains just now. He is one step removed from the drink slipper. The second type is dry, but his thinking is all "wet." He is intolerant, critical, and moralizing. He may well know Step 1, perhaps even Steps 2 and 3, but he has yet to dig into the meaning of Steps 4, 5, 6, and 7. The spiritual experience and the taking of stock in Steps 4 and 10 are still there for him to feel in depth.

The Desire to Stop Drinking

Do we want to drink more than we want not to drink? For example, Joe stops drinking to keep his job, to stop his wife's nagging, to get rid of his creditors' threats. These reasons are based on fear. Would Joe stop drinking if he had a million dollars? Would he quit if he had no other problems at all? Would he quit simply to enjoy the adventure of a more responsible, free life, to explore the mysteries he has always been afraid of? Would he stop for himself, for his own personal meaning? What is the purpose behind his desire to stop drinking? Does he intend to quench his personal thirst or his "conning" thirst.

As stated previously, every intention consists of a desire *and* a purpose. If the desire to stop drinking is harmonized with our primary purpose, to be sober, all is well, or as well as it can be. The strange fact is that we often have a lukewarm desire to stop but lack the purpose to be sober. The nature of the desire to stop drinking deepens in quality and sincerity directed by a loving act. We do not easily slip as long as we feel that sobriety is an act of love.

The compassion of Tradition 3 is a great blessing. We qualify as A.A. members simply by having a desire to stop drinking. Mercifully, the nature of that desire is not spelled out. Just a glimmer of a desire, just a lukewarm whim, will do at the start. The nature of the desire to stop drinking and to stay stopped depend on how we feel, why, what we want, and how we go about it. To really want to be sober, to realize our own best meaning, is a loving act. This way gradually the desire to stop drinking deepens so that, in fellowship, we lose the desire to drink.

But, tragically, to be dry on fear is to slip indefinitely. The slipping stops when we really want to be sober more than anything else in the world.

In response to personal thirst, the aim of sobriety is to want to be ourselves, to feel good for our own sake. This purpose is fueled by the desire to stop drinking, which becomes the desire for fellowship, and this quenches personal thirst.

From time to time we need to examine our thirst. Most often, an urge to drink is an urge to "drink in" some vital personal experience, far more urgent than the need for alcohol. It is the need for love, for fellowship, for a dialogue with those who understand.

Joe drinks because he wants to drink more than he wants not to. He is an upset man who drank, stopped drinking, but is drinking again. He has not gone much beyond Step 1. He could go on to drink himself to death with the grim alibi "I am sick and helpless." Step 1 is necessary but not sufficient; alone, it cannot bring sobriety. Joe must also reaffirm Traditions 3 and 6—desire and purpose.

When upset or disturbed, it is easy to slip. Then we should try to become aware of how we feel. The feelings most likely to spin us off are all related to ownership, control, and conquest. These feelings, which stem from the possession principle, include envy, resentment, jealousy, depression, self-pity, and loneliness. They arise when we find ourselves in competition with others.

Personal meaning is blocked when we compete with others. If we want to stay sober, we do not compare ourselves with others in the appraisal of how we are doing. We compare ourselves with ourselves. What new depth of meaning have we reached? Are we realizing our dream?

Friends, of course, are priceless exemplars, but we must not compete with them or try to make them over. We can be busy enough just being ourselves.

The question about a slip is, "What went wrong and what can I do about it?" The problem is mine if I slip. It is yours if you slip. We should avoid taking each other's inventory.

Sometimes one who slips makes better progress than a

dry, disgruntled person who is unhappy and tense. The tense individual is dry under pressure, not because he really wants to be sober.

How much do we want not to drink? If we do not want sobriety, we can never know it. We never value anything we do not want. If we do not value our sobriety, we can easily lose it.

A friend who slips proves something to us. His slip proves the truth of Steps 1 and 2—each of us is powerless over alcohol and can do nothing by himself.

There are four stages to recognize in the study of slips, and in the purpose of sobriety: (1) the effort to be sober, (2) the problem of addiction, (3) problem drinking, (4) early pleasant drinking.

In the effort to be sober, we note that reason is more important than cause. A reason is a basic ground for creative action. The effort to be sober is an effort to be free, grounded in a reason, not a cause.

We need also to note the distinction between reason and intention. We may have reason to be sober but not intend it or we may support it with an intention that may or may not work. We may have reason to feel good and do nothing about it. Or we may supplement the reason with an intention made up of a desire to drink and a purpose designed for drinking in a comfortable, safe, satisfying way. This is a self-design.

With the collapse of that self-design we may wish to fulfill our reason to feel good in another kind of intention that will combine the desire to stop drinking with the purpose of becoming sober and staying that way. The desire to stop drinking becomes a desire for fellowship. Coupled with the sober purpose, it is a personal design that works.

Reasons, then, are closely related to intentions. Both are more than drives, instincts, urges, or motives. Reasons and intentions always arise from the inner person, the acting "I," the creative center of personal action. They are not observable objectively; they can, however, be felt through personal know-how.

Reasons and intentions differ. Reasons can exist without intentions in action, and intentions can be carried on without reasons. We often have reasons to do things that we never act on, and many of us have often intended to drink for no reason except for the fun of it. This we have done more to explore life, to savor adventure, to romp in the unknown, than for any clear, specific reason. Kant, in his study of art, of esthetic feeling, made a purpose out of purposelessness!

Life is to be lived more for its mystery than for its mastery. However, rarely can we live this way all the time. We are beset by trouble and, when a problem faces us, we search for reasons. The basic reason of all, next to abandon and joy of living just for the fun of it, is found in the longing to feel good, to be ourselves as freely as possible. This personal thirst we quench with intentions that work. The central one is the intention of freedom. The reason, the longing to feel good, coupled with the intention of becoming free, forms the personal design for sobriety.

In the problem of addiction we find that cause is relevant. Cause is what we look for when something happens. There is no doubt that something happens in the course of drinking that was not intended, not chosen, not designed. In this area we may seek causes in chemistry, physics, physiology, pharmacology, or in any science that may throw light on what went wrong.

Problem drinking presents us with alibis. These excuses are used by the drinker to explain away action that he regrets or wishes to cover up.

When we find ourselves using alibis, we can know that we have lost the bulk of our freedom. Yet we are still barely free enough to choose our excuses and make our stories stick—for awhile. Then our alibi system collapses, and we realize that we turned to alibis when our freedom slipped away. This recognition comes through contact with others like ourselves, enabling us to accept the meaning of alibi use—defensive freedom, which is losing behavior. We may then intend to abandon it, if we choose, on behalf of our personal meaning and to reduce the possibility of a slip. Personal insight into alibis belongs to the effort to be sober, grounded in reason and intention, not in cause.

An insidious alibi often used is that since no one can find the cause for drinking, there is no use trying to be sober. "You may as well continue drinking," say these "con" men. Though plausible to some people, that alibi, of course, is ridiculous. Forms of cancer and the common cold are treated, often with success, though no one knows their causes.

While it is true that we strive to get beyond the alibis to greater freedom in creative sobriety, we should not regard alibi systems as denial or rejection. Alibis are a sign of loss of freedom, but they are also a desperate use of what remains of freedom. The use of alibis is a hopeful sign of something better to come. It is only when alibis have been used and then collapse that we thirst again for freedom. Out of that collapse will arise the capacity to find good reasons to be sober.

Confronted by a counselor who thinks we are slow in

facing our alibi talent, we will, of course, skillfully move out of his way. We do not wish to offend him, but our alibi talent is ours and we must discipline it in our own way. If we permit the counselor to take over, we lose what little freedom we have. Certainly we lose what we have if the counselor controls the way we move.

A.A. members do not confront a new candidate by exposing his defects, his defenses, his alibis. Rather, they present themselves to him: "Here is what I was like, here is what happened, and this is what I'm like now. You take it from there. Do with it what you can."

Recall of early pleasant drinking is another way we use to "con" ourselves into a drink. The nostaligic "good old days" may well lead us to a slip after we have been sober for a long time. We long for the pleasant early experience and think of it, time and again, in the vain hope that we may regain what we once knew in the golden dream days.

The memory of our early drinking days, when we enjoyed ourselves and felt no need for the support of excuses, is powerful enough to create an alibi enabling us to drink again.

However, if we use that memory creatively, it can become the reason to find early joy in the sobriety program. We should not try to blot out the pleasant memory of early drinking. We can use it productively in this belief: we stop drinking and become sober for the same reason we first drank, to feel good. The habit of wanting to feel good can be directed better by the personal design of sobriety than by a relapse into drinking.

The Futile Search for Cause

If we believe we had reason to drink and reason to be sober, we cannot call drinking and sobriety simply events that happen. To act on reason is to act with choice, even when the choice is limited by fear, as in an alibi.

The reason we have for anything we do can become an intention. One and the same reason—for example, to feel good—can give rise to two kinds of intention. The intention to drink is an intention of having. The intention to be sober is an intention of being.

Reason and intention figure chiefly in the early stage of drinking and throughout the sobriety program. A design is clearly in process in our early drinking days and in our sobriety.

Design is also at work in the sick, problem-ridden stage of our drinking. Here the form of design is cause. When something happens that we do not intend, something for which we have no reason, it is an event. We seek causes for events.

The event of addiction tells us we cannot drink. We did not intend to get sick, we had no reason to get sick. In this sense, addiction has a cause.

Two things stand clearly in the disorder of alcoholism —alcohol and damage. We do not know the cause, but we do know that drinking damages our lives in critical ways.

Our capacity for freedom in the search for reasons and intentions will bring us sobriety and insight into our trouble *where our choices do matter.*

Let us not worry about the cause picture. It is there, and scientists are working on it. Whatever they discover will be welcome. But only we can decide that we want to be sober and stay that way.

The search for cause, for insight into causal conditions, belongs to the "hard" sciences—the domain of the medical doctor and his research colleagues. This includes the psychologist, for his discipline is a biological science.

To use cause or to search for cause in everything is a form of blame placing. To seek cure, in the same spirit, is to seek control. And to seek control is to continue with the same problem we had as "controlled" drinkers. At best, we drank to loosen control; so there can be no cure and no value in seeking a cure.

To seek an "expert's" cure is to find someone who will explain the cause of the disorder and what to do about it. Such action reveals a deep dependence on authority—the authority of the expert and of the cause. It blocks our effort to understand and accept fellowship, a community of amateurs. Dependence on the expert is dependence on cause in two ways—dependence on the expert as the cause of our recovery and dependence on what he explains to us as the cause of our disorder. Both kinds of dependence can prolong drinking or lead to a slip. Instead of reliance on authority, we need to deepen respect for our personally conceived reasons and intentions as we cultivate the art of sobriety.

The Problem of Control

The worst thing to befall the art of feeling good is the habit of control, imposed on us either by ourselves or by well-meaning counselors. Such counselors I call control counselors because they put great stress on *loss of control.* Such loss, by implication, is regarded as bad, for one reason or another. And that is precisely why the alcoholic evades the confronting tactics of the control counselor and clings to his belief in control.

After all, he did exercise control for a long time. Even recently, when much of his control was lost, there were times when getting drunk did not mean trouble or sickness or when drinking did not even mean getting drunk. He could handle it at times if he tried a little harder. Actually he could believe that he never really lost all his control every time he drank. He just could not be sure, that is all. Control was uncertain, he could admit that. But gone, really gone?

The belief in control dies hard. Why? The alcoholic learned control from the same society that produced his counselor. He learned it from the fear of surrender, a humiliating experience he is urged to undergo by his control counselor. He is encouraged to admit his loss of control, surrender to a victorious God and a victorious counselor. In this way he will · magically demonstrate self-control, although he has just surrendered his capacity to control drinking.

So control is let in by the back door as a valuable experience in sobriety, in every area but drinking. According to this view, then, control is a commendable technique of personal choice making.

The control counselor refers to the patient's alibi pattern as a *denial system.* But his own negation of the patient's technique is itself a denial system! For what are attacks on alcoholism, either in education or in treatment, but denial systems?

The shame of loss of control is culture-based. No wonder the drinker, dry and fearful, clings tenaciously to control. His whole world tends to collapse when someone infers he has "lost his grip." But this need not happen if he is shown that control inhibits and cripples the life of freedom, joy, and adventure.

There is no need to confront a patient with his denial

system if we appreciate the value of his loss of control, if we recall that he drank in order to loosen control. If we can communicate without pressure, without confrontation, we tend to flourish in good will. If we fail to respect the value of loss of control to the patient, we deny him a feeling of creative meaning. This value is not in the need to be abstinent because he has lost a good thing and would regain it if he could. The value is more deeply rooted in the fact that *control itself is the problem.*

The use of control in search of cure and recovery, either by science or will power, is a sure sign of addiction, no matter where the drinker is—early, midway, or late in the drinking pattern. Questions about whether the control is successful, dubious, or useless do not matter. The problem is control. The therapist committed to the goal of self-control, the denial system concept, and the need to elicit from the patient an admission of loss of control is in as much trouble as the patient.

The need to drink is a more dramatic illustration of "powerless over alcohol" than loss of control. Having to drink is there before the individual—clear, urgent, definite. Loss of control is more evasive, harder to define, than the need or desire to drink. Moreover, few drinkers ever completely illustrate loss of control all the time.

The control counselor tends to neglect the way the drinker feels about the need to drink. Instead, he stresses loss of control as a sick event, a bad happening.

The drinker who is encouraged to think of loss of control as a desirable aim will respond freely and creatively. In the drinker's feeling, drunk or sober, the loss of control is an experience of abandon, of joy, of anonymous adventure. It is not necessarily a bad end-result of the addictive

process. This feeling can be brought into awareness if the
drinker is not confronted by the loss of control as a critical
experience. If he can be helped to understand his trouble
as the need, the urge, to drink and to use control in doing
so, he will get closer to the truth of the problem in a less
threatening way.

It is easier to help a patient recognize he is a successful
controller than a poor one. Then he may easily see that his
need for control and the use of it follow the loss of discipline and the loss of fun and joy of carefree living. If the
counselor abandons his control tools, he can explain that
discipline is what we cultivate to make us more free, more
creative. We only turn to control after we have lost discipline.

The lesson here for the A.A. member is "Don't push the
person you sponsor." Let him explain how well he controls his drinking. Then explain to him how you could
control your drinking and your life.

The loss of control is not as tragic as the loss of discipline, the loss of the fun, joy, and adventure of drinking.
The pressure of the desire to drink is much more important to discuss than the loss of control because in the
drinker's life something will have to replace the desire to
drink. That will be the desire for fellowship. The best way
to that desire will be to show the alcoholic that you appreciate his desire to drink, the need to feel good, more than
you need to confront him with the loss of control.

Contact, recognition, and acquaintance—the three features of personal know-how—are found in Steps 1, 2, and
3: acceptance, creative effort, and love. Acceptance of his
problem is what the denier needs. Creative effort is what
the alcohol fighter needs. And fellowship is what the loner
needs. It is important to recognize that denial, struggle,

and self-reliance are problems that may characterize both the patient and the therapist.

When we enjoy doing what we want, we always do it in concert with others, in fellowship. This experience is based on defect. When we relax with one another in discussion of defect, there is no fear.

Alcoholism is a pattern of fear, a love disorder, a lost art. We drank to change the way we felt because we wanted to feel better, in good will and affection. It is the same habit we cultivate in sobriety, except that we change the technique.

The slip or relapse is a failure in feeling good. It is funny that the only way we can get what we want out of drinking is to become free in sobriety!

It is a great mistake to think that another drug might help us feel good. Such thinking has led to countless slips. Let me review some drugs in common use and their dangers, including depressants, stimulants, and hallucinogens.

The depressants include the barbiturates and the tranquilizers, the bromides, and the narcotics. The phenothiazines are dangerous when potentiated by other drugs or when used too long and excessively. Likewise, the antihistamines can be abused with resultant harmful effects. Darvon, Librium and Valium are three drugs as commonly abused as barbituates or meprobamate.

Stimulants include nicotine, the amphetamines, cocaine, Benzedrex, Preludin, Wyamine sulphate, the MAO inhibitors, and antidepressants such as Tofranil and Elavil.

Harmful hallucinogens include belladonna alkaloids, scopolamine, phencyclidine, and tryptamine, used to synthesize other hallucinogens.

The use of drugs either to replace or potentiate the

effects of alcohol should be carefully avoided. Sometimes
the innocent taking of a drug for medicinal purposes can
help precipitate a drinking spree.

The Prospect of Love

The main feature of the slip problem is the deception
of pleasure, pain, and power. What do we really want out
of drinking or drugs, out of sobriety?

To be attracted to pleasurable feelings, to be repelled
by painful ones—these standards are not enough for lasting sobriety. It is, of course, good to be pleased and good
not to suffer needlessly; so we turn to ways of controlling
our life in order to be pleased and to be rid of pain. The
resort to control is as deep a habit with some counselors
as it is with patients. These are the counselors who press
for an admission of loss of control, who confront their
patients with their denial systems and urge them to surrender. It is clear that control here is highly regarded
presumably because such control may yield more pleasure and less pain. The control of drinking is allegedly
"surrendered" to God, the therapist, or the group. Just
what "they" do with it is not certain. Anyway the patient
is expected to develop control of his life in every area but
the one he has "surrendered."

However, control is an experience that does not fit into
the action of freedom. Discipline, yes, but not control.
Actually control limits and inhibits freedom because it is
always accompanied by fear.

Control cannot make us free and cannot make us loveworthy. We can avoid the contradiction between surrender of ability to drink and control in all other areas if we
abandon both the ideals of surrender and of control. In

their place we stress acceptance and discipline. Acceptance of our alcoholism makes more sense than surrender of ourselves, or some part of us, to who knows what. We need everything we have, alcoholism and all. With a little creative effort, the alcoholism can be directed into productive channels. The thirst will never die. We have only to learn to clarify our thirst and quench it productively.

Acceptance of our alcoholic nature and discipline of it in living as we want enables us to become free and resourceful in pursuit of love—a steady devotion to things that matter most. At best, love is a beautiful feeling of harmony, without the desire either to be pleased or to avoid pain. It is indeed pleasurable, but it is a pleasure the lack of which is not painful.

Without love, without the longing for love, we seek to be satisfied, but like broken bottles we can never be filled. Pleasure for itself can never be sated. That is a principle of addiction. Likewise the removal of pain in pursuit of pleasure belongs in the course of an addiction. The pursuit of pleasure, the avoidance of pain, the control exercised to bring on the one and to avoid the other, figure in the dynamics of control counseling. Such counseling fosters the very problem it seeks to alleviate.

Thirst is never quenched by drinking. When we drink or depend upon any other form of self-pleasure, we become empty as fast as we are filled. However, desires can be channeled into lasting joys when we make sure that what we want is what others want.

This sharing becomes the love of our life. It is a goal higher than pleasure or the avoidance of pain. When we put it in first place, we need never worry about pleasure or pain. We will be as pleased as we desire and as little distressed by pain as we could wish to be. There is no longer anything to fight, no conflict to endure, when we set our sights on freedom and the creative efforts of love.

The desire driving us to drink or to any possession is the same desire that will fuel our primary purpose—sobriety and the love that keeps us free. We can realize this through the miracle of fellowship.

As agents we are free. As artists we are creative. As friends we are lovers. As friends in the adventure of fellowship we learn to love and continue to be free and creative. All this is best pursued informally in the climate of anonymity.

Chapter 8

The Summing Up

Alcoholics Anonymous has a very sound program for teaching alcoholics how to be sober and stay that way. Unfortunately, A.A., together with all other treatment modalities, accounts for only about ten percent of all alcoholics on a program of sobriety.

The bulk of people who go to A.A. find real help. Once exposed to the program, the alcoholic does well. By his own admission, he only slips when he falls away from the practices of fellowship. Thus, A.A. works for those who work the program.

How can A.A. best attract the millions who still suffer from alcoholism? These people fall into three main classes: (1) authority-ridden people; (2) those who suspect that they should be able to break or control their habit; and (3) spiritually shy people. A.A. members must devise means to reach these three groups in a much better way than we commonly use now.

Authority-ridden people have a strong bias for prestige. It is hard for them to believe that other amateurs like themselves can be of real help. They keep looking for causes, cures, and experts who will do the job for them, without their personal involvement. Their problem is that they cannot respect fellow alcoholics because they cannot respect themselves.

We A.A. members who are professionals in any area should do more to attract these prestige-conscious people. At first such people will respond with respect because of their need to have "experts" on their side. Eventually, we will impress them more with the fact that we are alcoholic than with the fact that we are professionals.

In our communities we can make A.A. much more attractive by urging patients, students, and clients to try A.A. Our recommendations will be respected, especially if we are in A.A. Anonymity means freedom to counsel informally, and that is more important than concealing a "good" name.

Those who believe they must break or control their habit are, of course, alcohol fighters. The most revolutionary note to strike with such people is to tell them that they do not have to break or control their habit.

Before I joined A.A. the three things I feared most were the misery of hangovers, the prospect of indefinite abstinence, and my deep attachment to the unity I sought in alcohol. In all these fears there was no trace of a desire to stop drinking. Certainly alcohol made me sick and I had to stop drinking for periods at a time, but there was no thought of an enduring sobriety program. I loved drinking too much as a way of life to entertain any notion of ongoing sobriety.

What change made it possible for me to embrace A.A.? I really desired to stop drinking because "I was sick and tired of being sick and tired." That well-known sense of resignation is chorus of thousands of A.A. members. However, something more important than acceptance of my distress took hold of my life. I discovered, with great joy and relief, that I could go on wanting to feel as great as

I wanted to feel when I drank. *I did not have to control or break my habit.* There was nothing to fight, nothing to support, nothing to control, nothing to defend. I simply proposed to become sober with the same good intention I had when I started drinking—to be myself as well and as enjoyably as possible.

The third group of people that A.A. must attract are the spiritually shy people. Without any real knowledge of A.A., these people tend to regard A.A. as an evangelical venture, with conversion, Bible pounding, and lurid confession fests. They refuse to go to A.A. because they say they cannot take the spiritual angle. This "reason," though an alibi, is one we must face head-on. The way to meet it is by stressing that "spiritual" simply means "personal." To become a person is to be a human being who is free. To become a person is to learn that you cannot be free, creative, and loving by yourself. The mystery of personhood is that you need others to be you. That is all skeptics, agnostics, and atheists need to know at the start. Everyone deepens his meaning in a sobriety program. The spiritually shy may begin with a modest position.

The admission of self-powerlessness coupled with an open mind is all that an alcoholic needs in the spiritual area. Any or all spiritual beliefs are respected in A.A.

We can encourage millions of alcoholics to seek sobriety by convincing them that their alcoholism flourishes in the needs for support, control, and self-reliance. These needs do not cease in sobriety. They simply find healthier expressions and fulfillment in the skills of fellowship. A.A. members cooperate instead of compete, create instead of control, and love instead of withdraw.

The large number of people who are authority ridden,

alcohol fighting, or spiritually shy justify this study of the personal treatment of alcoholism.

A.A. stands strong in its own right. It needs no justification from the professional areas. However, as long as there are people with the fear of authority, the fear of fighting a habit, and the fear of the unknown there will be a need to approach them with insight into their special problems.

Everything in the personal treatment of alcoholism is in harmony with the A.A. program. The personal treatment is an effort to make the A.A. program available to more who still suffer. The desire to stop drinking must be made more attractive, for no one will go to A.A. or stay in it if he does not really desire to stop drinking.

Many more alcoholics will develop the desire to stop drinking and to stay sober if we band together and devote ourselves to the education of the three main classes of people who are not A.A. members.

What group of people is better able to carry on this education than we A.A. members who are professionals in medicine, science, psychology, law, and theology? We know the problems of authority, we have been confused in our basic beliefs, we have fought, striven to control, won and lost.

The people reluctant to try A.A. are like ourselves in more ways than we are, at first, aware of. There are many doctors, educators, scientists, lawyers, and clergymen among those who still suffer. There are still many more who, though not professional, think and feel as we do because of the values of the society we live in.

A program of the sort described in this study is, therefore, one of value as an adjunct to A.A., the kind of program that most professionals can both use and teach.

Throughout the study, the concept of personal know-how is designed to deal directly with the problems of authority, of habit, and of ultimate personal values.

Personal know-how is a buffer between organized society and the fellowship of A.A. There are millions so conditioned by authority, prestige, and control in society that they are not ready for the simple radical insights of A.A. Until A.A. finds a way to bring in those millions still in need of help, there will be a place for a program of the kind described in this study.

Suggested Readings

Alcoholism and Drug Use

Abel, Ernest L. *Drugs and Behavior.* New York: John Wiley and Sons, 1974.

Alcoholics Anonymous. *The A.A. Grapevine,* monthly magazine.

Anonymous. *Alcoholics Anonymous.* New York: Works Publishing Co., 1975.

Bateson, Gregory. *The Cybernetics of "Self": A Theory of Alcoholism. Psychiatry,* vol. 34, Feb. 1971.

Bell, R.G. *Escape from Addiction.* New York: McGraw-Hill, 1976.

Greenberg, Leon. *What the Body Does with Alcohol.* New Brunswick, N.J.: Rutgers University Press, 1975.

Jellinek, E. M. *The Disease Concept of Alcoholism.* New Haven, Conn.: Hill House Press, 1960.

Keller, Mark. *How Alcohol Affects the Body.* New Brunswick, N.J.: Rutgers University Press, 1975.

Keller and McCormick. *Dictionary of Words about Alcohol.* New Brunswick, N.J.: Rutgers University Press, 1975.

Kissin and Begleiter. *The Biology of Alcoholism,* vols. 1–3. New York: Plenum Publishers, 1973.

Lingeman, Richard. *Drugs, A to Z.* New York: McGraw-Hill, 1974.

Malcom, Andrew. *Pursuit of Intoxication.* New York: Washington Square Press, 1972.

National Council on Alcoholism. *Criteria for the Diagnosis of Alcoholism.* New York, 1973.

Ray, Oakley S. *Drugs, Society and Human Behavior.* St. Louis: Mosby Co., 1972

Rutgers University Press. *Journal of Alcohol Studies,* issued quarterly.

Stewart, David A., 1950. *Alcoholism as a Psychological Problem. Canadian Journal of Psychology,* 4:2.

————, 1951. *The Problem of Value in the Study of Alcoholism. Quar-*

terly Journal of Studies on Alcohol. Yale University, Sept.

————, 1954. *Empathy in the Group Therapy of Alcoholics. Journal of of Studies on Alcohol,* Yale University, March.

————, 1954. *Ethical aspects of the Group Therapy of Alcoholics. Journal of Studies on Alcohol,* Yale University, June.

————, 1955. *The Dynamics of Fellowship as Illustrated in Alcoholics Anonymous. Journal of Studies on Alcohol,* Yale University, June.

————, 1957. *The Meaning of Intoxication. Journal of Social Therapy,* vol. 3, 3.

————, 1958. *Through Thirst to Recovery. Journal of Social Therapy,* vol. 4, 3.

————, 1969. *Thirst for Freedom.* Center City, Minn.: Hazelden.

————, 1972. *How to Be a Better Boozer.* Palm Springs, Calif.: Empathy Books.

————, 1973. *High on a Dream.* Palm Springs, Calif.: Empathy Books.

————, 1974. *The Art of Feeling Good.* Brighton, Mich.: Brighton Foundation.

Weil, Andrew, *The Natural Mind.* Boston, Mass.: Houghton Mifflin, 1972.

Music, Creative Writing, and Criticism

Adorno, Theodor W. *Philosophy of Modern Music.* New York: Seabury Press, 1973

Aristotle. *On Poetry and Music,* ed. by S. H. Butcher. New York: Library of Liberal Arts, 1975.

Baum, P. F. *The Other Harmony of Prose.* Durham, N.C.: Duke University Press, 1952.

Camus, Albert. *The Stranger.* New York: Random House, 1954.

Copland, Aaron. *What to Listen for in Music.* New York: Mentor, 1957.

Crane, Stephen. *Maggie: A Girl of the Streets, & George's Mother.* Greenwich, Conn.: Fawcett, 1975.

Day, Douglas. *Malcolm Lowry.* New York: Oxford University Press, 1973.

Fitzgerald, F. Scott, 1945. *The Crackup.* New York: New Directions.

———, 1953. *The Great Gatsby.* New York: Scribners.

———, 1960. *Tender Is the Night.* New York: Scribners.

Frye, Northrop, 1947. *Fearful Symmetry.* Princeton, N. J.: Princeton University Press.

———, 1963. *Fables of Identity.* New York: Harcourt, Brace and World.

Goodman, Nelson. *Languages of Art.* New York: Bobbs, Merrill, 1968

Gross, Laila. *An Introduction to Literary Criticism.* New York: Capricorn Books, 1972.

Hough, Graham. *An Essay on Criticism.* New York: Norton, 1966.

Huxley, Aldous. 1960. *On Art and Artists.* New York: World Publishing Co.

———, 1963. *Literature and Science.* New York: Harper & Row.

Jackson, Charles. *Lost Weekend.* Paris, Tenn.: Manor House Press, 1973.

Keats, John. *Poems and Letters.* Boston, Mass.: Houghton Mifflin, 1899.

Kerr, Walter. *Tragedy and Comedy.* New York: Simon and Schuster, 1968.

Lowry, Malcolm. *Under the Volcano.* New York: Lippincott, 1965.

Lynch, W. F. *Christ and Apollo.* New York: Sheed and Ward, 1960.

McMullen, Roy. *Art, Influence and Alienation.* New York: Mentor, 1969.

McNamara, Eugene, ed. *The Literary Criticism of Marshall McLuhan.* New York: McGraw-Hill, 1969.

Newman, William S. *Understanding Music.* New York: Harper & Row, 1967.

Percy, Walker. *The Message in the Bottle.* New York: Farrar, Straus and Giroux, 1975.

Read, Herbert, 1963. *The Contrary Experience.* New York: Horizon Press.

———, 1967. *The Grass Roots of Art.* New York: Meridian.

Said, Edward W. *Beginnings.* New York: Basic Books, 1976.

Santayana, George, 1936. *The Last Puritan.* New York: Scribners.

——, 1961. *The Sense of Beauty.* New York: Macmillan.

Shakespeare, William. *The Tempest.* New York: Oxford University Press, 1969.

Trilling, Lionel. 1972. *Sincerity and Authenticity.* Cambridge: Harvard University Press.

——, 1973. *Mind in the Modern World.* New York: Viking Press.

Wordsworth, William. *The Prelude.* New York: Holt, Rinehart, 1954.

Zolla, Elemaire. *The Eclipse of the Intellectual,* tr. by Raymond Rosenthal. New York: Funk and Wagnalls, 1968.

Philosophy

Anscombe, G. E. *Intention.* Ithaca, N.Y.: Cornell University Press, 1966.

Aristotle. *Ethics,* tr. by Martin Ostwald. New York: Library of Liberal Arts, 1975.

Barrett, William. *Irrational Man.* New York: Doubleday, 1962.

Bergson, Henri, 1944. *Time in Western Philosophy,* from *Creative Evolution.* New York: Random House.

——, 1946. *An Introduction to Metaphysics,* from *Creative Mind.* New York: Philosophical Library.

Carritt. E.F. *Philosophies of Beauty.* Oxford: Oxford University Press, 1947.

Chomsky, Noam, 1972. *Problems of Knowledge and Freedom.* New York: Random House.

——, 1976. *Reflections on Language.* New York: Pantheon.

Coleman, Francis. *Aesthetics.* New York: McGraw-Hill, 1968.

de Chardin, Pierre Teilhard. *Let Me Explain.* New York: Harper & Row, 1970.

Hackforth, R. *Plato's Examination of Pleasure.* New York: Library of Liberal Arts, 1945.

Hampshire, Stuart. *Thought and Action.* New York: Viking Press, 1960.

Hartman, Geoffrey, H., ed. *Hopkins.* Englewood Cliffs, N.J.: Prentice-Hall, 1966.

Heinemann. *Existentialism and the Modern Predicament.* New York: Harper & Row, 1958.

Hofstadter, Albert. *Truth and Art.* New York: Minerva Press, 1968.

Kahler, Erich. *The Disintegration of Form in the Arts.* New York: Braziller, 1968.

Kaufmann, W., 1969. *Existentialism from Dostoevsky to Sartre.* New York: Meridian.

——, 1969. *Tragedy and Philosophy.* New York: Meridian.

Langer, Susanne, 1953. *Feeling and Form.* New York: Scribners.

——, 1957. *Problems of Art.* New York: Scribners.

Lauer, Quentin. *Phenomenology.* New York: Harper & Row, 1975.

Lonergan, Bernard. *Insight.* New York: Philosophical Library, 1957.

Macmurray, John, 1933. *Boundaries of Science.* London: Faber.

——, 1957. *The Self as Agent.* New York: Harper & Row.

——, 1961. *Persons in Relation.* London: Faber.

Marcel, Gabriel, 1961. *The Philosophy of Existentialism.* New York: Citadel Press.

——, 1964. *Creative Fidelity.* New York: Noonday Press.

Maritain, Jacques. *The Responsibility of the Artist.* New York: Scribners, 1960.

Murdoch, Iris. *Sovereignty of the Good.* London: Routledge and Kegan Paul, 1970.

New Testament. *St. Matthew* (Sermon on the Mount), King James version.

Oates, Joyce Carol. *The Edge of Impossibility (Tragic Forms).* Greenwich, Conn.: Fawcett, 1972.

Oates, Whitney J. *Plato's View of Art.* New York: Scribners, 1970.

Ogden, Richards, and Wood. *Foundations of Aesthetics.* New York: Haskell, 1974.

Old Testament. *Book of Job,* King James version.

Ortega y Gasset, José. *Phenomenology and Art,* tr. by Philip Silver. New York: Norton, 1975.

Plato, 1962. *Plato's Epistles,* tr. by G. R. Morrow. New York: Library of Liberal Arts.

———, 1965. *Phaedo,* tr. by R. Hackforth. New York: Library of Liberal Arts.

———, 1975. *Theaetetus,* tr. by F. M. Cornford. New York: Library of Liberal Arts.

Polanyi, Michael. *Personal Knowledge.* New York: Harper Torchbooks, 1964.

Ross, Sir David, ed. *Aristotle.* New York: Scribners, 1971.

Sadler, William. *Existence and Love.* New York: Scribners, 1969.

Saw, Ruth L. *Aesthetics.* New York: Anchor Books, 1971.

Stein, Edith. *On the Problem of Empathy.* The Hague: Martin Nijhoff, 1964.

Stewart, David A., 1949. *Naturalism and the Problem of Value. Queen's Quarterly,* Kingston, Canada.

———, 1956. *Preface to Empathy.* New York: Philosophical Library, 1956.

Weil, Simone, 1956. *The Notebooks.* London: Routledge and Kegan Paul.

———, 1971. *Waiting on God.* London: Collins.

Wilson, Colin. *The New Existentialism.* Boston: Houghton Mifflin, 1967.

Psychology

Bonner, Hubert. *On Being Mindful of Man.* Boston: Houghton Mifflin, 1965.

Brett, G. S. *History of Psychology,* ed. by R. S. Peters. Boston: M.I.T. Press, 1975.

Buhler and Allen. *Introduction to Humanistic Psychology.* Belmont, Calif.: Brooks Cole, 1972.

Campbell, Joseph. *The Mythic Image.* Princeton, N.J.: Princeton University Press, 1974.

Laing, R. D. *The Divided Self.* Baltimore: Penguin Books, 1975.

Riegel, K. F., ed. *The Development of Dialectical Operations.* New York: S. Karger, 1975.

Ryan, Thomas Arthur. *Intentional Behavior.* New York: Ronald Press, 1970.

Rychlak, J. F., ed. *Dialectics. Humanistic Rationale for Behavior and Development.* New York: S. Karger, 1976.

Stewart, David A., 1954. *The Psychogenesis of Empathy. Psychoanalytic Review,* July.

———, 1955. *Empathy, Common Ground of Ethics and Personality Theory. Psychoanalytic Review,* April.

———, 1966. *Money, Power and Sex.* New York: Libra.

Suttie, Ian. *The Origins of Love and Hate.* Baltimore: Penguin Books, 1963.

Taylor, Leone E. *Design for a Hopeful Psychology. The American Psychologist,* Dec. 1973.